The Pastor's Start-Up Manual

BOOKS IN THE LEADERSHIP INSIGHT SERIES

LEADERSHIP LIS INSIGHT SERIES
LEADERSHIP LIS INSIGHT SERIES
LEADERSHIP LIS INSIGHT SERIES

The Pastor's Start-Up Manual

Beginning a New Pastorate

HERB MILLER, EDITOR

A moment of insight is worth a lifetime of experience

ROBERT H. RAMEY, JR.

Abingdon Press
Nashville

THE PASTOR'S START-UP MANUAL

Copyright © 1995 by Abingdon Press

This book is printed on recycled, acid-free paper.

Library of Congress Cataloging-in-Publication Data

Ramey, Robert H., 1929–
    The pastor's start-up manual: beginning a new pastorate/Robert
H. Ramey, Jr.: Herb Miller, editor.
       p.   cm.—(Leadership insight series)
    Includes bibliographical references.
    ISBN 0-687-01486-7 (pbk.: alk. paper)
    1. Clergy—Office.   2. Clergy—Appointment, call, and election.
3. Clergy—Family relationships.   4. Pastoral theology.   I. Miller,
Herb.   II. Title.   III. Series.
BV660.2.R344   1995
253—dc20

95-16971
CIP

Scripture quotations, unless otherwise indicated, are from the New Revised Standard Version Bible, copyright © 1989, by the Division of Christian Education of the National Council of the Churches of Christ in the United States of America.

00 01 02 03 04 — 10 9 8 7 6 5

MANUFACTURED IN THE UNITED STATES OF AMERICA

To
Robbin,
Garry,
and
Andrea:
my three children,
who moved often,
complained a little,
endured well,
and
who now encourage me greatly!

ACKNOWLEDGMENTS

No one ever writes a book without tapping the expertise of countless people, or without presuming upon the goodness of family and friends. Certainly this book is no exception; therefore, I want to thank the principal contributors to *The Pastor's Start-Up Manual.*

I am grateful to the trustees, administration, and faculty of Columbia Theological Seminary for granting me a sabbatical leave in the winter and spring of 1994 to work on this book. I want to thank President Douglas W. Oldenburg in particular for his strong support of my work.

As I wrote the book, I became grateful once again to the five churches that formed the crucible in which my approach to ministry was tested before I started teaching ministry at Columbia Seminary. I refer to White Memorial Presbyterian Church, Raleigh, N.C.; St. Andrew Presbyterian Church, Lynchburg, Va.; Knox Presbyterian Church, Norfolk, Va.; Selwyn Avenue Presbyterian Church, Charlotte, N.C.; and Memorial Drive Presbyterian Church, Stone Mountain, Ga.

As I wrote, I also became aware of how much I owe to seminary students in our various degree programs. Through their feedback and our interaction on ministry issues, I learned much. A number of those students surface herein.

I want to thank Cynthia Gadsden and David Ellis of Abingdon Press who worked with me during the tedious editing phases of the book. Herb

Miller and Paul Franklyn also provided much support as the basic format developed.

Finally, I am grateful to my wife, Gail, who encouraged me enormously in my writing. My three children, Robbin, Garry, and Andrea, to whom I dedicated the book, proved remarkably patient and understanding when my writing deprived us of some quality time together.

Soon some of my "insights" will be discarded. However, I hope that at least a few of them are on the mark. The persons named above contributed much to the insights that have enduring value.

FOREWORD

The first job for every pastor is to accurately define reality in his or her congregation and community. The second job is to exhibit a personal behavior pattern that fits this church's needs at this time in its history. The third job is to help people set an energizing vision for the future regarding what God calls this congregation to be and do. The fourth job is to patiently keep on keeping on while people cross the Red Sea of obstacles that always lies between today and tomorrow.

A pastor's ability to accomplish these four ministry tasks is to a major extent determined by his or her first year in the congregation. If the initial lap around the track goes poorly, other laps become irrelevant. Robert Ramey has significantly reduced the confusion inherent in getting out of the starting blocks. He brings together in a skillful way (1) a broad knowledge of how to do pastoral ministry in churches of every size, and (2) insights from the best practical ministry literature.

The early Greeks called the residence of powerful men a *kurikon,* based on a slang expression for *power.* The term passed into the Latin, and early Christians began using it to describe their meeting place—God's house. When Christian missionaries traveled into the Upper Rhine wilderness in the second century, they carried this word—*kurika* or *kurikon*—with them. By the thirteenth century, modern spellings had appeared, the closest to the original of which is the word *kirk* in Scotland.

Churches that live up to their potential deserve their original Greek label. They are places of power, capable of transforming human life and helping hurting people. Ramey provides interesting, practical suggestions for pastors who want to live out their first few months in a new congregation in ways likely to facilitate that result.

—Herb Miller, Lubbock, Texas

CONTENTS

INTRODUCTION

ANTICIPATING A
NEW PASTORATE

W hat are your fears, needs, and concerns as you now look toward beginning a new pastorate?"

A group of ministers and seminary seniors pondered my question as they sat around a table during a spring continuing education course. Eight ministers, each of whom was planning to move to a new pastorate, had returned for a five day refresher course on "New Pastorate Start-Up." I had also invited a small group of seminary seniors to participate since they were beginning not only a new pastorate but their first pastorate as well. Would not the two groups raise questions of mutual benefit? Moreover, I knew the seniors would benefit from hearing ministers who were moving to their second or third pastorates. I was not disappointed, for soon answers to my question poured forth in a torrent.

Obviously eager to begin, Jerry said, "In my first pastorate, almost as soon as I got there, one member began to challenge me, particularly on matters of race and sex. Once in a Sunday prayer I prayed for an end to racism and sexism in our society, and after the service this member said quite pointedly, 'Jerry, you'll do fine here as long as you remember not to deal with social or political issues. Don't even pray about them. You won't last long if you do.' Now by no means am I a flaming liberal, but I lasted only one year at that church. I've finally gotten another call, but I'm wondering whether the same thing will happen to me again. Can one dare be prophetic in this kind of world? And just how do we best deal with change and conflict?"

"That scares me," said Bill. "I'm ex-military. I've invested a lot of money and energy in this second career. Coming to seminary has proved very costly for me. In fact, all the money I've saved is about gone. Sometimes when I think about going to my first pastorate, I want to back away. Have I made the right decision? Have I heard God's call correctly? Suppose I fail? I simply can't begin again, not at age 47."

"I've got similar concerns but along a different line," said Susan, a young married student. "Last week I received a call as an associate. This church has never had an associate before. What will it be like to be the *first* associate? And will I be able to engage in a meaningful ministry there? I've heard some real horror stories about associates who left their first pastorates within a year. A friend of mine, for example, worked with a minister who used all the right words about team ministry when she interviewed with the church. Actually, though, control was the big issue for him. He didn't want her to do anything significant, like baptizing babies. She couldn't take it any longer and soon left. I don't want the same thing to happen to me!"

"I'm excited about going to my second church," said Stan, "but I have a confession to make. I went to my present pastorate simply because it was my only option. I intended to stay there only long enough to establish myself in ministry, and then to move on to a more promising church. Looking back, I can see that I wasn't fair to my congregation. While I can't undo the past, I do want to put down some deep roots when we move to a new community next month. I need some guidance on how to do that."

Frank, a young seminary senior, said, "I know this will sound stupid, especially with so many veteran ministers here, but I'll ask my question anyway. What do I do when I first get to a church? Really, what do I do? Set up my office? Make visits? Start planning my first service? Talk with church leaders? Maybe it will come to me, but I want some suggestions about how to get started in ministry."

"I think that some of us 'veterans' can help you a little with that, Frank," laughed Mary. "But that doesn't mean we have all the answers. Take me, for example. I became involved in so many church and community activities that I finally decided to move in order to get some relief! I never learned how to structure my time in my first pastorate. I've simply got to do a better job of personal maintenance the next time around. And I need some help with that issue."

Heather, a studious senior who seemed to have it all together, said, "I've been thinking about all the things I will have to do for the first time, like attending board meetings. I can talk about liberation theology and contextualization, but I feel inadequate when it comes to the 'nitty-gritty' of daily parish life!"

So went the fears, needs, and concerns of that group composed of practicing ministers plus seminary seniors, all of whom intended to begin a new pastorate soon. Their concerns, plus others I will mention, have prompted this book. Space constraints of course permit me to answer only some of the most important questions about beginning a pastorate.

Even so, what I have written must remain more suggestive than definitive. For every new situation into which a minister moves is unique. Each congregation has its particular identity and context, its own programs and ways of doing things. And surely each minister is also unique! No book could ever apply to all the nuances of every pastoral relationship. Yet, are there not general principles that will apply to many, if not most situations? I have written this book in that belief.

My background in ministry should help with the task before us. A colleague humorously reminded me that I was no expert in this field since I had only begun my ministry once. Though he was exactly right, I have begun a new phase of my ministry six times. I served in the pastoral ministry in five different churches, including service as an assistant pastor, as organizing pastor for a new suburban church, as pastor of a declining inner city church, as pastor of a stable neighborhood church, and finally as pastor of a rapidly growing suburban church. For the last sixteen years I have served as professor of ministry at Columbia Theological Seminary, teaching basic and advanced courses in ministry, administration, polity, conflict management, and spiritual formation. Those theological students and the five churches I served have been my real teachers. I will therefore draw upon our mutual ministry as I answer basic questions ministers and students have raised about moving to a new pastorate.

The reader will quickly note that I do not fully address such basic matters as models of the church and the theology of mission. While these subjects are crucial for ministry, I am assuming that anyone reading the book will have been thoroughly grounded in them elsewhere. My own understanding of these matters will surface of course throughout the book, but I will not dwell on them.

Though I will discuss the needs, roles, and skills of *ministers* from cover to cover, my intention is to point toward an ecclesial paradigm. In other words, *the goal for any minister in beginning a new pastorate is to lead the church as the people of God to be a sign, foretaste, and instrument of God's reign.* Thus I will encourage the minister to develop not only individual skills—preaching, teaching, counseling—but also the interpersonal and group skills required to lead a congregation in ministry and mission.

By writing about various fears, concerns, and problems involved in a new pastorate start-up, I may seem to be painting a negative picture of ministry. That's not my intention. In fact, I don't believe that any vocation is more challenging and exciting than pastoral ministry. Those of us with many years of experience in ministry can testify that it's an awesome responsibility and privilege to preach the gospel, sit with the bereaved, guide a church in its worship and work, talk with children about God, help laity discover their ministry in the world, and enable people to find resources for growing in their faith. Never would I want any concern or fear about ministry to squelch the excitement of the gospel.

Though discouraged and embroiled in conflict many times, so far I have not suffered burnout. Though often afraid to apply the word of God to a specific crisis, I have been able to overcome my fear most of the time. Simply put, the One who called me *to* ministry has sustained me *in* ministry. And many others as well. Even those who have gone through the trials of burnout or been victimized in church disputes have often come back to enjoy the most productive years of their ministry. For God has renewed their strength. Perhaps they never climbed the proverbial ministerial ladder as high as they once dreamed, but they were faithful and effective nonetheless. Sometimes they labored beneath tall steeples in great metropolitan areas, sometimes in blighted areas of the inner city, and sometimes in the lovely frame buildings that dot the countryside. But wherever they labored, they did not labor in vain.

So, to the task! Whether you are starting up in your first church or third, ministry beckons.

CHAPTER 1

STARTING UP

We begin with the important question Frank raised in the introduction, "What do I do when I first move?" He was honestly puzzled about what to do when he arrives in his new pastorate. How Frank answers this question the first few months in his new congregation may determine his effectiveness in that particular church. In fact, the first two or three years in ministry for any seminary graduate will drastically influence his or her future career. Is it not therefore important for Frank to begin wisely and well?

But it's no less important for Jerry, Stan, and Mary to begin wisely and well as they move to another pastorate. What they do in the early months will also seriously affect the ministry that follows.

Starting Up as Family Member

I'll admit I nearly botched my entry into several parishes by simply being too eager to start working. Now those congregations didn't necessarily think I blundered; they probably thought I was energetic and committed. Still, I failed my family. How? I was so anxious to begin my work that I neglected to help them enter *their* new situation. I should have known better. After all, I knew that people would have more opportunities to welcome and get to know me than they would my family.

So, if I had to do it over again, I would spend more time at home, unpacking the china, taking my children to school, and doing little chores that would have eased all of us into a new situation.

Fortunately, I did learn from my start-up mistakes. By the time I moved to my last parish, I requested that I not be asked to preach the first Sunday I was there. During most of the first week I settled in with my family, unpacked, opened a bank account, and ran errands. And when that first Sunday rolled around, my family and I visited a church of another denomination in the community. Only then did I begin work. And it resulted in a much better entry for all of us.

Your start-up in your pastorate may be quite different from my experience in my fifth pastorate. You may have to preach your first Sunday. You may be single and *want* to start work sooner. Still, I would unpack my books last if I were beginning my ministry now. You first need to get oriented in your home and community. And that is the kind of space most churches will give you. Later you will spend plenty of time at the church, perhaps more than you wish! In the beginning, if you have a family, don't fail them. They need your help in their new surroundings.

Starting Up as Worship Leader

Plan your first church service carefully. Even those members who have only a mild interest in the church will want to meet you and hear your first sermon. They will form a definite impression of you, sometimes an impression that will never change. Does that mean you should make sweeping changes in the order of worship to demonstrate your freedom and creativity? No. Such a move would cause some members to fear that you were going to turn the parish upside down. Never mind what some may have told you about wanting many changes in the liturgy; stick to the old order of worship at first. Although you retain the identical order of worship the congregation is used to, you can enrich it with your own distinctive approach. Your prayers will be different, your sermon will be different, your announcements will be different. Let your identity, therefore, be reflected in the way you conduct and flesh out the liturgy, not in innovation. Plan any changes later with your leaders.

What sermon do you preach at the first service? Certainly not your heresies or your wildest ideas for changing the world. Preach on a text that allows you to express your deepest convictions about the gospel. Your initial task is to establish a relationship with the congregation that has placed its trust in you. So a sermon that demonstrates what anchors you in and to the faith will build that relationship. When you illustrate your sermon, keep in mind the various age groups in the congregation. Of course, you can't be all things to all people in every sermon, but surely in your first sermon you will want to identify with different groups. Intentionally ask yourself, for example, how the content of the sermon will play with the youth and the baby boomers, as well as the senior citizens.   **x**

As a matter of personal curiosity, I checked my early sermons in a congregation where I began as an assistant pastor. I discovered I had dealt with those themes I had struggled with in college and seminary—the mystery of suffering, the power of the cross, the person of Christ, and the nature of love. Those sermons introduced me to the congregation, because members could see how the gospel had informed and empowered my life. That gave the sermons a reality I hoped would build a solid relationship with the congregation. In later pastoral moves I relied on old standbys for the first few weeks—it's difficult to write new sermons when you arrive! And I always included one sermon on the nature of my ministry plus one on the ministry of the laity.

Another strong possibility for your initial sermon is to preach from the lectionary, that is, if lectionary preaching is your intention. You can introduce the congregation to your style by using the lectionary texts and adapting them as necessary for a new beginning. I didn't start my ministry by preaching from the lectionary, but were I to commence my ministry now I would soon begin to do so, if not the first Sunday. Though it has some disadvantages, lectionary preaching has the great advantage of providing congregations with the length, breadth, height, and depth of the gospel. It also focuses the attention of the congregation on the texts themselves more than on you and your struggles. And we must admit that some people may not find our experiences as interesting as we think.

Inevitably, how you meet the congregation that first Sunday will depend on you. Above all, be careful not to be condescending or critical of the culture you are entering. Two associate pastors moved from the North to the South and began work at about the same time in the same church. One greeted his new congregation this way: "Hi, y'all! Guess I've got to put on my best Southerneese today." The reaction was predictably negative.

However, the other associate simply said, "When I was a girl growing up in the North, we canceled Sunday school in the summer and had one worship service. Perhaps we did so because it was cold for so long that we wanted to have more time outdoors! But I really like the fact that you have both Sunday school and morning worship here during the summer." And the people said, "Amen!"

As "transition technologists" have told us, you will make your entry into the parish much the same way you entered your last social engagement.[1] At that time did you plunge right in, introduce yourself to strangers, and make small talk? Or did you sit in a corner and wait for someone to come over and speak to you?

In parish life, as in your social engagements, how you relate expresses your basic personhood. For example, after your first sermon picture yourself standing in the church entrance, waiting anxiously and hopefully as people start filing out. In your mental picture, are you taking the initiative to meet people, find out who they are, and show them you are glad to meet them? Or are you standing to one side, waiting for them to approach you? If the latter, you need to approach them, even if you are normally retiring or shy.

Yet, how you meet people when you start up involves far more than describing extroverts and introverts. Ministers have to fill a *role* of being friendly and approachable whether they are basically outgoing or not. So let people know that you want to establish a strong relationship with them. If you don't do that in the beginning, parishioners may not give you another chance. This doesn't mean superficially glad handing everybody and becoming a "hail fellow, well met." But relating to people does involve seeking them out, looking them in the eye, shaking hands warmly, and showing that you care about them. Unfortunately, we are seldom able to undo the first impressions we make—we are stuck with them. So, as you meet people in your new parish, consider how you relate to them. Whether you meet them at your first service of worship, the grocery store, or Little League practice, meet them well!

Design your installation service with care. Perhaps you will be ordained, then installed to office. Awed by the nature of ordination and empowered by the Spirit, you well may tremble as hands are laid on you and the prayer of ordination is offered.

If you are moving to a second, third, or fourth pastorate, you will only need to be installed. And you will also be awed by the mystery of God's call as you are officially installed. Either way you begin can be a powerful experience for you and your congregation.

Scheduling that important service will depend, of course, on various denominational practices. Whenever it's scheduled, enable the congregation to grasp the significance of the occasion. If you are being ordained, many of your members will never have shared in the ordination of a minister. So help them see that you are being ordained for the church universal, not just for your particular denomination.

Because polities vary so much, I cannot provide you with a suggested order of worship. Check your denominational book of worship. However, all services should contain special music, strong preaching, and wide participation. I'll never forget being installed in my fourth church with a former moderator of our General Assembly preaching and several trumpets accompanying the choir. May your service sound the theme that you are there to equip the saints for the work of ministry, not to do ministry all by yourself.

When permitted in your tradition, you may want to invite people from outside your judicatory to take part. If they do, ask your board to defray any travel expenses outside participants may have. Of course, some churches will be on tight budgets and find this impossible. Yet don't take for granted the services of other persons. Also take into account their need for lodging and meals while they are in your community.

A word of advice: whenever you can, schedule your service at the principal hour your church worships. As one who takes part in frequent ordination and installation services, it has usually seemed to me that services scheduled in the afternoon or evening have less vitality and fewer people in attendance than those scheduled during a regular morning service. Nonetheless, a morning service is not always possible, because ministers whom you would like to invite may have to conduct services in their own churches.

A second word of advice: apprise the various participants of the need for brevity. Most services contain charges to the minister and the congregation, as well as a sermon and special music. Also, the one presiding normally explains the nature of the occasion, particularly if ordination is involved. As a result these services can drag on far too long and exhaust even your family and friends. That's unnecessary, especially if your service of worship is scheduled as a special Sunday service. Keep it brief!

Culminate your special day with a reception for everyone. The reception further broadens the opportunity for others to celebrate your arrival. What a wonderful time for the congregation to come forward and welcome their new pastor or associate pastor. But avoid elaborate arrangements that prevent those who prepare the reception from being present for the service.

However you work out the details for your ordination and/or installation, celebrate it with your congregation. Make it the special occasion it is!

Starting Up as Pastor

Relationships, relationships! Nothing is more important for you during your early months than establishing relationships with your congregation. How you build relationships will partly depend on the size of your congregation. What you do to establish relationships will vary greatly from a 50-member church to a 250-member church to a 500-member church or to a multiple staff position in an 800-member church.

Regardless of the size of the church, however, do four things. First, find out who is in the hospital and go to visit them immediately. Though your visit should never be a ploy to curry favor, your action will send a clear signal to the congregation that you intend to be an attentive, caring pastor. But beware, you have to continue to be a pastor to reinforce the pastoral identity you establish.

Second, ask who the shut-ins are in the congregation and go to visit them soon. You will thereby visit those who cannot take the initiative to meet you. You can also serve them communion whenever the sacrament is served in the church. A clergy couple reported to me that they had asked who the shut-ins were in their parish, as I had once suggested in a seminary class. Strangely, no one told them about two members who were confined to their homes. Only much later did the clergy couple find out about them, but by then the shut-ins were feeling quite neglected. So, with knowledgeable members to assist you, go over the church rolls, one family at a time, and note the level of activity in each family. You may therefore be able to take due notice of everyone.

Third, visit all those in the congregation who have recently been bereaved. No doubt they are still struggling with their grief and may miss the previous pastor on whom they leaned for comfort and strength. While you can't fill the previous pastor's shoes, you can begin to build a helpful relationship with those in grief. You can also broaden this category of visits to cover all those who have suffered a painful loss of any kind: those newly separated or divorced, those whose children have moved out on their own, those who have lost their jobs, those who have retired, or those who have lost power. While they may be reluctant to confide in you so soon, your visit will let them know you care.

Beyond these visits, inquire about others who may need pastoral concern. Obviously, the larger the congregation the more time it will take you to make all of the calls. But as you phase them in, you will discover one of the great blessings of ministry: being welcomed into the lives of your parishioners—their joys and sorrows, their successes and failures. So heed the counsel of Paul who said, "Rejoice with those who rejoice, weep with those who weep" (Rom. 12:15).

Now you are ready to visit people who have no known problem requiring pastoral attention. In a small church of 50 members, the members are probably clustered in only a few families. Small churches by nature want someone to care for them, so it will be necessary for you to visit them often. And with only a small number of families to care for, you can spend more time with them.

However, if you receive a call to a church of 250 members, the congregation will likely be much more diverse. Of course you won't be able to visit the members as soon or as often as in the 50-member church. You will also be drawn into the administrative tasks of the church, for your leadership will be needed more in that context. One strategy, therefore, is to invite different groups of people to your home until you have gone through the entire congregation. Share the story of your call with them—yes, one more time! And ask them to share their experience in the church with you and the group.

In this entire visitation process, begin to visit the inactive members. There are always some inactive members in every congregation who are anxious for a new beginning. For reasons perhaps unknown to others, they may have had difficulty relating to the previous pastor. Or they may have had a crisis in their lives and felt neglected by the church. Or again they may have slowly lapsed into inactivity and are now looking for any excuse to return. Your visit may be just the catalyst they need to rejoin their church family once more.

If you are an associate engaged in multiple staff ministry, your job description may specify certain groups for you to visit. As an illustration, if youth ministry is your assigned work, visit the homes of the youth. Also, contact the youth leaders and the Christian Education Committee members. Perhaps it would help for the church to sponsor a hamburger cookout one Sunday evening for the youth, their families, and their leaders.

During these early days of your ministry in a new congregation, you may be surprised by how few people come to you for counseling. And if you are young, they may come even more slowly. Yes, those who are really hurting or who have been deeply scarred will approach you, but others will likely hold back. They want to see whether you are a caring, vulnerable, approachable, trustworthy person before they share their pain with you. But I found that when I persistently showed the congregation I cared, they began to come—sometimes faster than I desired! Yet their slowness in coming will be good for you initially, because you need to do many essential tasks as you begin your ministry. Thus, by the time they ask increasingly for help, you will be well-grounded in your work.

Starting Up as Administrator

Some ministers curse church administration. Surveys indicate that most ministers rank preaching, teaching, and pastoral care above administration both in the importance of the task and their own enjoyment of doing the task. But don't let such statistics leave a bad taste in your mouth for administration. Administration has received a bad rap, one that is ill-informed and undeserved. While it may never be your favorite ministerial task, you can nonetheless do it purposefully, even enthusiastically.

The following metaphor will help you look at administration differently. See yourself as a navigator on a ship guiding the congregation in ministry and mission to God's intended destination. As you guide the congregation, you will be concerned about building up the body of Christ, as well as launching the body in mission to the world. To do so, you will need to see that administration *is* ministry. It's not just preparation for ministry, nor something you have to get out of the way so that at last you can do ministry. No, it *is* ministry.

When you give theological guidance to a group working on a church mission statement, that's ministry. When you guide the people of God to do their work in the world faithfully and effectively, that's ministry. When you help a committee not only to perform its tasks well but also to become sensitive to the needs of committee members, that's ministry. Once you adopt this attitude toward administration, you'll find it less boring and much more exciting. It will challenge you to give your best to guide the "ship" in the direction God wants it to go. And, once again, such guiding *is* ministry.

But how do you get started in administration? Your key co-laborers will of course be your staff and church leaders. Yet you may say, "What staff? I'm it!" Still, you will likely have some secretarial help, if only on a part-time or volunteer basis. And you will also work with people who lead your music program, care for the church building and grounds, and keep the church books. *With whatever staff you have, build a team.*

Your staff will be very eager to find out what working with you is like. And they will also want to know how they can please you. Follow Sidney J. Spain's advice when he suggests that you ask each staff member "to write a detailed job description of what they now do, what schedule they follow, and to whom they report. Ask 'how you can help them'—what the deadlines are for sermon titles and newsletter material, and who picks the hymn numbers."[2]

Assure your staff that you want to work with them. To back up your assurance, spend time with them individually and also as a group if the staff is large enough. As you do so, share with them what your needs are, your schedule and day(s) off, your personal style, your work deadlines, and your wishes about confidential parish information. And by all means let your secretary know your approximate schedule each day, especially when you will be at the church.

Your work with your church board will also be crucial. A board that is dead set against you and your ministry will frustrate and block you at every turn. After all, they have power and outnumber you! So work with them, not *around* them. Work with them, not *against* them. Work with them, not *without* them. Be prepared to guide them and initiate proposals as needed, but bear in mind that your ultimate goal is to equip them for the work of ministry. And they will watch your leadership style very carefully. It may contrast sharply with their own style or with your predecessor's, but if your intention is to equip them for ministry, stick to it patiently and lovingly. Leadership has a tremendous "trickle down" effect. For people tend to emulate the behavior of their leaders!

Facing your board for the first time is difficult not only for beginning ministers but for seasoned pastors as well. The following suggestions may help you get off to a good start.

1. *Read previous board minutes to apprise yourself of what has been done in the past, both actions taken and how they were recorded.*
2. *Talk over past board meetings with a trusted member or members.*
3. *At the outset of the first meeting, ask if board members can take a few minutes to share some of their hopes and dreams for the church.*
4. *Ask board members, if relevant, to offer suggestions for improving your meetings.*
5. *Discuss with your board your desire for meetings to be fulfilling for them personally as well as productive for the church.*
6. *Ground your work together in love for God and neighbor as you have experienced it in Jesus Christ.*
7. *Assure your board members that you will be praying for them every day, and ask them to pray for you.*

In addition to meeting with board members in regularly scheduled meetings, meet with them individually as often as you can. If convenient and appropriate, visit them where they work. Ask them about their work in the world as well as about their work in the church. As you take an interest in them and support them, you model the kind of helpful, supportive leadership you want them to display as they work with their committees and in other areas of their lives. Remember, when you meet with your leaders you are building personal and working relationships without which you can accomplish little.

Generally it's helpful to meet with every committee you'll be working with in the church. When you meet with your key leaders, as suggested above, you pave the way for attending your first committee meetings. Miss no opportunity to be present at their meetings, taking notes and asking questions. You will probably be expected to attend anyway as an advisory member. Yet when you attend, tell them you are there to learn what they do and how they do it. Refuse to jump into the role of "Reverend Fix-it," thereby relieving them of the responsibility for working with you on the problems. Rather, as the Center for Parish Development suggests, begin to develop a problem-solving climate within the church.[3] With such a climate, pastor and people can work together in ministry.

How do you build a problem-solving climate? By trusting people, showing that you welcome new ideas, offering supportive behavior, expecting them to do their best, demonstrating a helpful spirit, and using group input to make decisions. But how tempting it is to take shortcuts by doing things *for* the congregation instead of *with* them! Though empowering and equipping them will take longer to effect changes, such leadership will have a more lasting impact on the church.

Nonetheless, are there not some tasks that always seem to need attention in every church? Yes, and as long as you do not violate the principle of building a problem-solving climate, you can address some of the church's specific tasks. Lyle E. Schaller, for example, has listed seven questions he thinks pastors should ask when going to new congregations. Keep in mind, however, that if you are going to your *first* pastorate, you may not have the background in ministry to address these seven questions quickly. Even so, Schaller's questions will help, especially if you are a proactive type and can hardly wait to swing into action! Here they are:

1. How are the finances here?
2. What is the procedure for inviting visitors?
3. Who are the returnees? (Since I came as pastor.)
4. Who are the dropouts? (Since I came as pastor.)
5. Who are our prospective new members?
6. What are the most distinctive assets and strengths of this congregation?
7. What are the staffing needs here?[4]

To Schaller's list, I would add at least one more question: where are people hurting in this community? If nothing else, this question focuses the attention of people on the mission of the church outside its walls. The other questions deal only with building up the church. While you can have little mission to those outside if the church is floundering internally, you want people to begin to grasp the church's *total* mission. Question 8 will move them in that direction.

Again, by raising these questions, don't convey that you intend to address them unilaterally. Ask leaders and members for their input as you seek solutions. A collaborative leadership style will result in greater mission accomplishment and also in better personal relationships.

Starting Up

Starting up with your congregation as worship leader, pastor, and administrator is crucial, as you can see. Yet, even while you are starting up in these roles, a story continues to unfold: your story, the members' story, and the congregation's story. Understanding this evolving narrative will yield many benefits. The next chapter shows why.

CHAPTER 2

TELLING STORIES

The discussion in our New Pastorate Start-Up Seminar began to heat up one day when Alicia said, "How personal can we get with a congregation in sermons—I mean, like telling about our own experiences? A minister once told me we should never do that."

"I see it quite differently," said Jerry. "People need to know we are human too. And I always perk up and listen more attentively when ministers share their own experiences."

"And how can we expect people to tell their stories if we never tell ours?" added Stan. "I've found that when I risk being vulnerable other people seem to open up more."

Alicia put an important question on the table that day. Yet her question has even broader implications than whether ministers should relate their own experiences in sermons. It also applies to parishioners, all of whom have their stories to tell. Moreover, the congregation itself has its own story that has slowly evolved during its history.

Actually, telling you my story reveals my identity, it indicates who I am. When I tell you the story of my call to ministry, for example, I am disclosing how God personally tapped me on the shoulder. When a parishioner tells me how she became a computer programmer, she is indicating how she feels God is calling her to use her talents to meet the world's needs. And when a congregation becomes aware of an exciting chapter in its history, its members see, more clearly than before, who God is calling them to be corporately as the body of Christ.

Of course, we only catch glimpses of who we are through the stories we tell. As pastor and people trust one another more fully, they pull their masks aside a little more. That's what building a relationship with a congregation is all about. Without mutual self-disclosure plus congregational disclosure, pastor and people can never grow in their relationship. Telling our stories can do much to build a deeper relationship.

Revealing Your Story

No minister can be effective without growing in self-awareness, without engaging in the process of self-understanding. When we pull aside the masks we wear, we see the person we truly are, rather than the person we present to others.

Tragically, some ministers cannot stand the discomfort of looking within. Yet when they refuse, they gradually become hollow and secretive. Over the years I have known many of them. They still preach, but not convincingly. They give pastoral care, but perfunctorily. Always they keep you at arm's length, for if they cannot look at themselves, neither will they let you see them as they are. And their ministry suffers, though people somehow never quite know why.

Thus, as a minister, be aware of your personhood. Move toward self-disclosure and away from secretiveness. For, as someone has said, you are only as healthy as your secrets.

Does that ever mean disclosing yourself fully to a congregation? No. That could prove disastrous, as some ministers have discovered. But it does mean being honest about yourself with a selected group or therapist. Such honesty, developed in an atmosphere of trust, acceptance, and confidentiality, will permeate your preaching, your pastoral care, and your administration. People will be drawn to you, for they will sense that you are an authentic human being who models the faith you preach and teach. Such authenticity is basic for the strong relationship you seek to build with your congregation.

Whenever you preach, people are more likely to listen because you will speak from *your* heart to *their* hearts. They will respect and trust you more. Should you use personal sermon illustrations? Certainly, as long as they enhance the sermon, and as long as you remember the words of Paul,

"For we do not proclaim ourselves; we proclaim Jesus Christ as Lord" (2 Cor. 4:5). Also, be aware that you can disclose more about yourself than you should. Whatever your decision about using personal illustrations, observe a deeper point. When you are an authentic, honest, growing person, you will embody a note of reality in your ministry that will enrich every pastoral function. Those who grow in the private, inner recesses of their hearts will make their public faces much more authentic.

How and where can you find such a nurturing relationship? A support group of trusted colleagues can fill that need for you. A periodic relation- ✗ ship with a therapist can keep you honest and growing. A strong relation-ship with your spouse, family, and friends is crucial. Belonging to a sharing group or having a spiritual director can also provide invaluable help. *However you choose to stay human, do it.* Those who seek to build mature relationships with others must keep their own hearts honest and open.

The nature of ministry is such that we must tell our stories from time to time. In our seminary's continuing education program, we invite graduates who have been out of school for two or three years to return and examine what has happened to them since graduation. When con-ducting the session on sharing joys and sorrows, I usually have to do no more than say, "Let's divide up into three's and share our joys first. Then we will come back together and get a report from the triads." Next, I do the same for their sorrows. Their stories of joy, pain, excitement, and confusion are always incredible to me. Obviously, ministry for them has not been quite what they had expected. Their ministries have been filled with surprises and frustrations. But what also becomes obvious as the three day experience unfolds is the remarkable power that lies in peer groups for healing and wholeness. When ministers are given the oppor-tunity to be honest about what is happening in their lives, it's often like a refreshing ocean breeze for them.

Listening to Others' Stories

Every member of every congregation also has a story to tell. When I began my ministry, I didn't know much about what I've been relating to you about starting up. But because of the good seminary training I received in pastoral care, I believed that a lot of suffering lay hidden behind many a calm exterior. I knew that parishioners, like ministers, live much of their lives behind a facade, revealing only so much. That very facade invites you to be attentive, to care, and to be patient. I knew that crises would cause their stories to gush forth. But how could I enable people to tell their stories in the absence of a crisis? All that we have discussed about ministers telling their stories paves the way for parishioners to tell theirs. If ministers are willing to be vulnerable, and if they have found healing for their own pain, then members will more likely share their lives.

Routine pastoral calling still affords a helpful context where stories can be told. Of course, amid rapid societal change, with more and more homes empty during the day, pastoral calling can be increasingly difficult. Yet whenever and wherever visiting is possible, stories can be told and ministers can use those stories to enrich their understanding of the human condition.

On these initial visits as a beginning minister in the parish, ask members to share their history in the church. Non-threatening questions, to which you respond sensitively, sometimes lead to greater disclosure. If that disclosure does not occur then, perhaps it will later. Often people will test you to see whether you can handle little things. Secretly many of them long to have a listening presence. Once they see that *you* are that presence, then they may trust you with the deeper material of their lives. Though that seldom happens all at once, routine calling sets the stage for it.

Small groups furnish another context for people to tell their stories. While some in every church will never like small groups, a significant number will. When a climate of trust and openness is established, people feel free to talk about their lives.

In working with persons in retreat settings and workshops, I often ask them to take a reflective look at their spiritual growth. I ask them to draw up three columns headed by the words "people," "events," and "direct experiences." Under the people column, I tell them to list the names of the people in their lives who have had an impact on them for Christ. I also ask them to reflect on what those people were like, what qualities they embodied. Under the events column, I suggest that they think about the circumstances of their lives—tragedies, anxiety-provoking events, and other crises—and discover how Christ came to them with power. Finally, under the direct experiences column, I invite them to write down any special times in their lives when God came to them in their prayers, Bible study, or church services.[1]

Help people move beyond dwelling on the problem to recognizing Christ's power to meet and work through the problem to develop a deeper relationship w/ God and w/ others.

Telling Stories

Then, in small groups and a plenary session, we talk about the people, events, and direct experiences that have enabled them to grow in faith. True, we don't hear the whole story of anybody's life; yet we hear more than enough to see how Christ has been at work among them. Frequently this exercise serves as a powerful stimulus to faith, both for the participants and me.

Can anyone minister effectively without staying in touch with the stories others have to tell? Surely no one can prepare vital sermons in a relationship vacuum. It's no more possible than attempting to minister without being aware of what's going on in your own life. Neither story is complete without the other. But once *both* stories are known, your ministry in all of its facets will be enriched. You will be speaking and living as a struggling human being among other struggling human beings.

Learning the Congregation's Story

You have a story to tell, each member has a story to tell, and each congregation has a story to tell. The late James F. Hopewell helped us understand the stories that congregations tell.[2] He exposed us to the drama contained in every church, a drama consisting of acts or stages, as well as plots that twist and turn. Through its story a congregation reveals its identity. One will not discover the church's identity merely by going back over the written record alone. Such written records may be replete with bare-bones details about when buildings were built and pastors came and went. However, such details will not yield the richness encompassed by the church's life. To comprehend that richness requires much additional work.

Thus, as a new minister in a congregation you will become a historian, but more than a compiler of dates and statistics. A former student, Harold, shared with me a series of reflections on his first year in a small southern church. One of the initial roles he assumed was that of becoming a "historian." He had learned well from Carl S. Dudley's *Making the Small Church Effective,* a book he read in seminary. Dudley stressed the conserving role of small churches. They are not against change, but do believe that conserving the past is a greater priority. Though history may not be as great a strength in the life of large or new congregations, it is in small churches.[3]

So Harold, our pastor-historian, went to work to find out what he could learn. With his particular congregation, founded in 1801, much golden history was waiting to be mined! And mine gold he did. During that first year he set out to discover as much of the church's history as he could. He also learned early on that "Small churches often have short memories." Therefore, they need help in order to recall past accomplishments.

When Harold began visiting during the early months of his ministry, he discovered that most of his parishioners were still hurting from the church's recent problems. Conflict and heartbreak had been the result of the tenure of their previous minister. People wanted to express their pain over those traumatic events, so the new pastor heard their stories. But Harold wisely invited them to go back even further and tell him other stories they remembered. That exercise considerably broadened their perspective.

The pastor-historian's strategy was insightful for another reason. "When people do not feel good about themselves or the church," Harold noted, "it's extremely helpful to have some pleasant memories and times to recall."[4] Those pleasant memories freed his church from being stuck in the recent past and helped them to eventually look toward the future.

Harold quickly became disappointed that there was not a greater collection of pictures and stories in a central place. So he began to mention his desire for "archives." Slowly but surely the congregation recognized his desire for historical material to be a genuine request. One member located a picture of the church before it moved to its present location. Another contributed some stationery that was printed before the porch and steeple had been added. Harold put all those fragments of history together for a bulletin insert one Sunday. He also turned the event into a children's sermon. One of the pictures he had collected was "fuzzy." So he talked about how our history can become fuzzy if we don't preserve it, and also about how our relationship with Jesus Christ can become fuzzy.

A further result occurred in the ministry of our pastor-historian. Through his careful historical work, Harold helped the congregation see that changes had taken place in their church. Therefore, change was still possible! Looking back, a natural tendency for small churches, had allowed them to celebrate their heritage. But looking back had also enabled them to turn and look forward to a church that would be 200 years old in a few short years.

Yet a pastor surely should not be the only historian in the church. Church members themselves should be vitally involved in telling the ecclesial story. Note again that when the church tells its story, it is describing far more than recorded dates and membership statistics. Those who compile such a history can use dates and statistics, of course, but the church needs much more to set forth its identity and to tell the church, community, and world who it is. How then can your church weave together all of the strands of its multi-faceted life?

James P. Wind, drawing upon contemporary congregational studies, likens the task to reconstructing a body.[5] To do so, the church must put together its many parts and bring them to life.

Basic to reconstructing the body is the skeletal framework on which the rest of the body fits. The familiar and popular time line can be drawn of the church's history. On newsprint or a chalkboard a group of church members can put together a tri-level history showing (1) what was happening in the church; (2) what was happening in the city or region; and finally (3) what was happening in the world.

In the process of building the time line, churches make valuable discoveries. Sometimes they learn that much valuable information has been lost. For example, I heard a group say the main reason they had previously called a woman to their pastorate was because they could get one cheaper! Such an unflattering and disturbing comment would never have been recorded in the church's official history but nonetheless provided a revealing glimpse into the congregation's psyche.

At other times participants in the time line process discover discrepancies between the oral and written versions of their church history. The written history may show the membership rolls at an all-time high, but the members themselves may feel that the church is actually declining. At any rate a time line enriches and expands a church's self-understanding.

After constructing the skeleton, look at the "organs" of the church. They are the ideas, beliefs, traditions, and values that called it into life and sustained it. One way to begin this process is to do a theological inventory of the congregation. Although the inventory provides only a present understanding of the church's major beliefs, it's still an understanding that is linked with the past. Persons will want to find, if possible, how the present theological climate is both similar to and different from the past, as determined from their other studies of the church.

Telling Stories

What about the "muscles and flesh" of the church? In this category are the congregation's major activities through the years including programs, ministries, building construction, customs, and controversies. Congregations are often embarrassed by their controversies, sometimes to the point of not even knowing they have any! Once during an interview with a woman in New York whose singing career was ended by a stove explosion, I asked how her church usually handled conflict. Looking somewhat puzzled, she said, "I'm not aware of any conflicts in our church." I think she was being honest, but did her statement also indicate the presence of a "no conflict" norm among key church leaders and members? Yet the content of church controversies illumines the strategic decisions a church has made, and such content should be brought to light.

Lastly, the body must come to life and begin to breathe. To initiate "the breath of life," Wind proposes identifying how the congregation has experienced the gospel. That means noting "parched spiritual times in its life and those when new life burst forth within it."[6] The purpose of the exercise is to enable people to make connections between the story of the Christian faith and the stories of their lives. By telling stories that forge those links, the living tradition of the church becomes strong and healthy. When people gather and make sense of their history, they are stirred to discover who they are in today's world and what they are called to do and be.

Obviously as a new pastor you cannot become such a perceptive historian all at once! Only over a period of years can you tell your story, hear the stories of the people, and learn the church's story as well. But no one ever said that a meaningful ministry could be developed overnight. Ministry is much more of a story that unfolds as you and your congregation live and love and learn together. And that takes time.

While you are telling your respective stories, you are doing so in a church whose size affects its dynamics. To function with increasing effectiveness, you need to understand thoroughly the dynamics of your particular church. Ignoring this facet of the entry process is a serious mistake, as the following chapter will demonstrate.

CHAPTER 3

RESEARCHING
YOUR CONGREGATION

I came from a large, 2,000-member church," Anne said in our seminar one day. "That's all I've ever known. But now, after considering my call options, I've decided to go to a 100-member church in western Kentucky. What differences am I likely to note? I know I can't use the same leadership style I've seen pastors use in large churches!"

Anne raised a vital question for our discussion. Many seminary graduates grow up in large churches, yet begin and end their ministries in small churches. One seminary in my own denomination advertises its role in theological education this way: "75% of all theological students come from churches of 1,000 or more members. 90% of all pastors serve churches of 250 or less."[1] Obviously, small membership churches have different expectations about pastoral leadership than do large membership churches.

Church consultants use different typologies to describe the size and dynamics of various churches.[2] In all of their proposed schemata, they employ different numbers of members or worshipers to categorize and explain churches. Perhaps it makes more sense to classify churches by the average number of *worshipers* in attendance on Sunday rather than by the number of members on the church roll. After all, churches and denominations use varying criteria for reporting their membership numbers and for determining who stays on their rolls. The simplest way to describe churches is from three viewpoints, *small, medium,* and *large.* It is beyond the scope of this book to deal with so-called mega churches.

What follows are basically accurate descriptions of three churches; however, the names of churches, pastors, and locations have been changed. The lenses these churches provide for studying congregations can help as you tiptoe through the tricky maze of pastoral leadership.

Crossroads Church

Upon graduating from seminary, Cynthia accepted a call to Crossroads Church, located in a small town of 1,100 in central Missouri. Erected in 1896, the church building has served the community continuously throughout the years. The facilities have not been greatly changed except for the addition of central air conditioning and heating, plus a few minor alterations of several doors. The one tiny, unventilated bathroom, in the basement, is inaccessible during the Sunday school hour due to its location.

The sanctuary, an attractive and historic building, is large enough to seat 100 people. However, attendance at Sunday services averages only 25 out of a membership of 51 people listed on the active church rolls. Crossroads has no choir. Cynthia says her singing is not inspired but that she sings with all the gusto she can muster! Furthermore, she has become painfully aware of the importance of music in the worship of God. "What a wonderful gift it is to those who are so blessed," she affirmed in personal correspondence with me. "I pray that God will send someone here who has the gift of music and is willing to share that gift."

Of the 51 persons listed on the active church roll, twelve of them carry the surname Smith. Of these twelve persons, three are named Sarah. Thus there are three Sarah Smiths, as well as another woman named Sarah. "As you might imagine," Cynthia writes, "this has caused me some confusion!" "Add to this," she continued, "the absolutely baffling kinship structure of the church, plus the fact that I have been advised on good authority not to ask too many questions, and you begin to catch a sense of my dilemma."

As Cynthia probed the kinship structure of the church more deeply, she discovered that eighty-five percent of the congregation was related to the Smith family. She had already learned that one of the characteristics of the small church is its single cell structure.[3] Soon she recognized that the single cell structure at Crossroads was further complicated because it was a single *family* cell church! Thus Cynthia wondered whether the congregation could ever absorb new members who moved into the community.

Describing a typical Sunday morning, Cynthia said, "It was something of a shock to discover that folks start showing up for Sunday school at about five after ten and trickle in thereafter. If I begin the worship service at eleven sharp, which I intend to do, then half the people are not there yet. I have never encountered this before. It seems that time isn't as rigidly observed here as in other places I've been. That's hard on me because I'm somewhat of a stickler for punctuality."

Soon after Cynthia began her ministry at Crossroads, she started a "Minute for Mission" time in the service to highlight the denomination's program. That caused a disruption in the usual agenda of the service. "By the reaction you would have thought the roof had caved in," she said. "It took me three tries to get everyone to sit down and accept the fact that we were going to skip a hymn. Of course, I know what 'the book' says about tampering with entrenched tradition, and, believe me, I do respect that. Still, I felt that we needed exposure to the program of the denomination. And we are going to start that each Sunday."

"I wonder what it would take," Cynthia continued, "to change anything in the status quo. And frankly, some changes are needed if this church is going to attract new members!"

Aware that what she had written so far sounded negative, Cynthia concluded by saying, "Actually, I am having the time of my life. I love it. And as I visit and spend time with the folks, the pieces of the puzzle fall into place one by one. The reason I share all of this with you is to give you a feel for my situation here."

Crossroads Church, of course, does not accurately depict every small church with fewer than 100 worshipers in attendance at Sunday worship. But note some of the similarities Cynthia had observed immediately:

—the building, though large enough for worship, had poor bathroom facilities, probably indicating limited finances;
—the church was basically composed of only a few families (and mostly one family);
—the music program was quite deficient;
—the church was having difficulty attracting new members;
—the church strongly resisted a change in its Sunday worship, yet some changes were obviously necessary for it to survive;

39

—and Cynthia, though clearly nurtured in a different ethos, *loved her ministry.*

By no means does this brief description of Crossroads Church portray all of the dynamics involved in a small church ministry. For example, as Cynthia is already discovering, *relationships* will always be more important than *programs* at Crossroads. Also hinted at but not described is the fact that matriarchs and patriarchs from the Smith family are in a central leadership position. The congregation does not expect Cynthia to stress the future and lead the church in new directions. For her to get caught in a showdown with the parental figures early in her ministry would be to covet a quick move to other pastures. The Crossroads family wants someone to love them, not to take them in a different direction. Nonetheless, the challenge for Cynthia, for Crossroads, and for every small membership church will be to begin to say, "God has a new plan for us. Our best years of ministry are today and in the future."[4]

Now, members of Crossroads may complain about the patriarchs and matriarchs, but Cynthia should beware. If she starts a war with them, those members will side with the parental figures, not her. The members know that the parental figures will be there long after Cynthia is gone, and they will still be calling the shots. She should not dare them to fire at her!

Though some may shudder to read this, Roy Oswald states that the worst place a new graduate can go right out of seminary is to a church like Crossroads.[5] Why? They have a thousand ideas and theories they have carefully honed by writing dozens of scholarly papers for professors, most of whom live far from Crossroads Church. And they want to put those ideas to work right away by starting various programs, as did Cynthia. To be sure, the parishioners may attend her programs a time or two but usually become frustrated. After all, they don't want someone to come in and tell them how to run their family. Instead, they want someone to be their friend: to love them, visit them, and sit by their side when they hurt. *Pastoral care, therefore, is the most important skill ministers need in that context.*

If you cannot adapt to this expected leadership and pastoral role, you will probably be dissatisfied serving a small, family church. In fact, many such churches have pastors who stay only a few years at most. And actually they don't expect you to stay very long. Everyone else has always made a speedy exit, so why should you be any different?

But if you are already headed toward a small, family church, don't despair. Talk with your judicatory officials about ministry in the small church. Read several books on the nature of such ministry. Also attend a conference on the small church, and learn how to identify and work with parental figures. Talk with pastors of similar small churches. And if you unlearn much of what you may have learned about leading large churches, you just may have the time of your life!

A minister in a Doctor of Ministry course told an amazing story. When he and his family returned from their summer vacation, his next door neighbor came over and said, "Preacher, your hot water heater has a leak. Thought you ought to know."

Stunned, the minister asked, "How did you know that?"

His neighbor replied, "Oh, for many years we've had a key to the parsonage. Whenever the preacher goes on vacation, we look after it."

No doubt the minister was *still* stunned after that explanation. Even so he later said to me, "I never want to serve any other church than a small church." Yet the small church that is like a family is different and requires a different kind of pastoral leadership than St. Paul's Church, the middle-sized church we next consider.

St. Paul's Church

After serving one small town church in Pennsylvania, Carlos accepted a call from St. Paul's Church, situated in another small Pennsylvania town. St. Paul's was founded in 1827 and the lovely church building occupies a prominent place on one of the main streets leading into the town square.

With Carlos's strong leadership, St. Paul's is now averaging 110 worshipers on Sunday mornings out of 158 members on the active church roll. Both attendance and membership are steadily increasing at Sunday school and morning worship. Carlos preaches powerful sermons, and the choir provides outstanding music for a middle-sized church. In fact the combination of dynamic preaching and excellent music have led growing numbers of visitors to attend services at St. Paul's.

The growth and excitement in the congregation are leading to some "good" problems, however. The large choir overflows its space in the sanctuary and leaders wonder how to remedy the situation. The increased attendance has filled the eleven o'clock service to capacity. The leaders are thus wondering whether the church should now plan to expand to two services.

The fellowship hall, moreover, is much too small to accommodate the congregation at its Wednesday night dinners. And the church nursery, presently located on the second floor, is difficult to access and probably not in conformity with the town's building code. Sunday school classes have to meet in cramped quarters. And office space is also at a premium, although Carlos does have a small study.

In light of its growing membership and activities, the governing board of St. Paul's has made some significant decisions. It first appointed a Long Range Planning Committee to expand church facilities and address the need for more fellowship and educational space. The board also charged the committee to develop some goals and objectives for mission and outreach, as well as for spirituality. In yet another action the board has asked a professor from a nearby seminary to consult with them as they seek to carry out their task.

The Long Range Planning Committee has promptly seen that the church cannot start pouring concrete for a new building until it decides how it will be used. This discovery is pushing them to look at their overall mission as a church, their strengths and weaknesses, and how they should expand their programs. They are also realizing that they must involve the members in the planning process, not only to receive their input but also to motivate them to support any future building plans.

As the committee has met, its members have identified St. Paul's dynamic worship, relational groups, leadership resources, and participatory decision making as the church's greatest strengths.[6] Mentioned again and again has been the church's love for members of their church family. One member of the Long Range Planning Committee said, "Love is at the heart of who we are, and we never want to lose that quality."

St. Paul's position as a middle-sized church forms a marked and illuminating contrast to Crossroads, the small family church. By tracking the differences between the two churches, you can examine some of the leadership and pastoral demands you face if you move to a similar parish.

Note, first of all, that the average number of worshipers attending services at St. Paul's is 110 versus 25 at Crossroads. Lyle Schaller says that small churches have up to 100 worshipers present compared to 100 to 200 for the middle-sized congregation.[7] Clearly both churches fall within the

Callahan

parameters he set for their classification, thus forming the basis for further comparisons.

Next, observe that St. Paul's is characterized by dynamic worship. Unlike Crossroads, which is rattling around in its sanctuary space, St. Paul's is considering whether to expand to two services. Recall that Crossroads has almost no music program, leading Cynthia to covet a musician who will share the gift of music with them. St. Paul's, on the other hand, has an outstanding music program that the church wants to expand.

What is expected of the pastor as leader is also different in the two churches. Cynthia has discovered that Crossroads wants her to be a friend, a "lover," to use Carl Dudley's phrase.[8] The families of this small congregation want and expect her to be in their homes often. They do not want her to initiate new programs or lead them into the future. The matriarchs and patriarchs of the Smith family will provide all the leadership Crossroads wants or needs.

The situation at St. Paul's, however, is both similar to and different from the expectations of pastoral leadership at Crossroads. The members do want Carlos to visit more, as indicated in the low rating the Long Range Planning Committee gave their visitation program, which also measures lay visitation. At the same time the governing board realizes and expects Carlos to furnish strong, initiating leadership as they move together into a new future. No patriarchs and matriarchs control the decisions at St. Paul's; as a result Carlos now occupies the central leadership position, along with a few key leaders on the governing board. Carlos is finding that he has to delegate authority and responsibility to others, for he cannot do everything. He therefore has to depend increasingly on the committees to do their jobs.

Thus Carlos faces a growing dilemma. He senses that he needs to visit more and that the congregation wants him to visit more. Moreover, he knows that he must be available as the chief source of strength and comfort for his congregation in critical moments like illness and death. So he is trapped between having to initiate more leadership and needing to provide spiritual and pastoral support for the members. The demands on his time are beginning to overwhelm him. Were it not for his previous experience in one pastorate he would find it even more difficult. He does have a "barrel" of sermons and some pastoral experience to fall back on.

Also, his previous service as a military officer steadies him in face of his time pressures.

Yet another point of comparison between Crossroads and St. Paul's is instructive. Beyond question Crossroads is a family church, almost a *one* family church. It can hardly think of itself in any other way. The love of members for one another is obvious, and they expect Cynthia to care about the family also.

Not surprisingly, St. Paul's also regards itself as a family. Almost every one of the 158 members knows everyone else, at least by face if not by name. This characteristic gives the congregation a warm feeling about itself. But now they realize that the church is growing larger almost every Sunday. That's exciting to the congregation but also scary. In other words, it inspires them to see their growth, yet alarms them to think they might lose the warm, intimate feeling they have as new faces increasingly appear.

Both the congregation at St. Paul's and Carlos now have to make some difficult choices. As for the congregation, it will have to decide whether it will see itself in the future as a "congregation of *congregations* of circles, choirs, classes, and other face-to-face groups," as Schaller puts it.[9] That will surely be the price they have to pay for continued growth. And St. Paul's has not yet fully made that decision.

For Carlos the decision will be whether to keep on trying to meet all the spiritual and pastoral needs of the congregation as he is now doing, or to move toward increased staffing. If the latter is chosen he will no longer be able to be as interpersonally involved as he has been before because of his increased administrative demands. At this point Carlos seems willing to make that switch, since he and the governing board are considering employing a youth minister on a part-time basis.

One other observation about the middle-sized church deserves comment. Schaller contends that middle-sized churches vary tremendously— no two are alike. He says they are most easily distinguished by their distinctive personalities and that their ministry must be designed to fit their unique characteristics.[10] So consider the middle-sized church you are serving or considering in light of its individual distinctiveness.

The vast majority of mainline Protestant congregations are either small or middle-sized churches. This fact portends enormous consequences for your career as a minister. If you define success in ministry by being pastor of a larger church, you may be doomed to disappointment. There simply are not enough large churches to go around! But if you have strong interpersonal skills, like to be at the center of church life, and have an outgoing personality, then you may well be happy in a middle-sized church for your entire career.

Though few new pastors will serve a large church as head of staff, some will. Many more will serve on the staff of a large church. Still others may move to a large church by the time they make their second or third move. Therefore, a review of the dynamics of Trinity Church should help if you are moving to a large church context.

Trinity Church

Kevin, after finishing his Master of Divinity degree at a seminary in the eastern United States, accepted a call to become the first associate on the staff of Trinity Church, located in a growing North Carolina town of 8,000. Kevin was intrigued at the thought of serving in a different part of the country, particularly in a historic church like Trinity. His major responsibilities included coordinating the youth and Christian education programs, giving pastoral care along with the senior pastor, serving as liturgist in the Sunday services, preaching once a month, and staffing both the Christian Education Committee and the diaconate.

As with many seminary graduates who become associates, Kevin does not intend to remain an associate throughout his career. One factor about the Trinity call that most interested him was the prospect of working with Jacob, the head of staff.

Jacob, though he had previously served only one church, had chosen ministry as a second career. Before coming to Trinity, he had been in middle management in a large clothing store.

Unknown to Jacob, Kevin had checked on him thoroughly with other ministers and judicatory officials in the community. All of them described Jacob as mature, rock-solid, and fair—qualities Kevin knew he would need in a senior pastor if he were to thrive in a multiple staff situation. They further told him they thought Jacob's stability and experience would provide a collegial framework in which both of them could grow. But one of them did say that being the first associate might be more difficult than coming on staff later.

Founded in 1843, Trinity Church thus celebrated its sesquicentennial anniversary in 1993. With 498 members on the active roll, the congregation averages a total of 280 worshipers at its two Sunday services. (For our discussion, any church averaging over 200 worshipers can be classified as a large church.)

At the sesquicentennial celebration a speaker noted that Trinity is a church that thrives in a crisis. In 1986 a disastrous fire swept through the educational and fellowship building, either destroying or rendering unusable the entire wing. But the church, inspired by a new motto, "Our Time to Grow," rebounded quickly and in 1987 built a new facility consisting of 21,000 square feet.

The new Trinity motto proved accurate, for Trinity is growing in all phases of its life. In the fall of 1992, in conjunction with plans for the church's sesquicentennial celebration, the governing board of Trinity authorized a comprehensive mission study to guide the church in the third millennium. The study envisioned exploring in depth the church's calling from God, as well as its identity, context, programs, and processes. The board also appointed a dynamic CEO of one of the local industries to oversee the project and asked Kevin to serve as "local project coordinator." Though Kevin did not realize at the time of his call that he might be asked to assume such a responsibility, he gladly accepted, saying, "It ought to help me learn how to conduct a mission study." In one further action the board authorized the hiring of a consultant to steer the church through the planning process.

The mission study proceeded with only a few glitches and was completed in the early summer of 1993. The chairperson, who enlisted strong division leaders for the study, provided outstanding overall leadership. Moreover, Kevin worked tirelessly to coordinate the project at the local level, receiving strong commendation from the board for his efforts. After adopting the final report of the mission study committee, the governing board expressed appreciation for the committee's work and made plans to implement the goals and objectives.

Upon analysis, the above information yields important information about the nature of large churches. In 1987 when the church adopted its new motto, "Our Time to Grow," the membership was 381. By 1994 the membership had climbed to 498, representing a 30 percent growth. The point is that the church made a conscious decision to grow, because it did not want to stay a middle-sized church. For the church to grow, the pastoral leaders had to be committed to the principle of growth. If they had still been locked into thinking of Trinity as a small or middle-sized church, featuring strong interpersonal communication and pastoral and spiritual direction from the pastors, few changes would have occurred.

Of course, interpersonal communication is still needed at Trinity! But the pastors, Jacob and Kevin, now communicate much more with church leaders—recruiting, delegating, supervising, and evaluating. Says Arlin Rothauge, in commenting on the very large church, "The patriarchs and matriarchs return, but now as the governing boards who formally, not just informally, control the life of and the future of the congregation."[11] The pastors at Trinity know they cannot do it all and must work with the leaders. As a result lay leaders are providing a dazzling array of programs, ranging from delivering meals on wheels to senior citizens to sponsoring an appreciation service for local police and firefighters.

The congregation may not see either pastor in their homes as often as they did when the church was smaller. Thus the congregation *as a whole* will have to engage in meeting spiritual and pastoral needs. Trinity is fulfilling this function by training Stephen Ministers to assist the pastors in meeting pastoral needs. Moreover, the committees themselves, though basically task oriented, nonetheless manage to provide ongoing pastoral care for many of the members. Now the personal relationships of members at Trinity tend to form around small groups, the choir, circles, Sunday school classes, and mission groups.

Note another key feature of Trinity Church: its growing staff. In addition to Jacob and Kevin, the church also employs two people in music, a church secretary, a financial secretary, a hospitality director who handles the needs of indigents, a custodian, and a weekday kindergarten director. The staff, working with key church leaders, will increasingly set the tone for the church. While neither Jacob nor Kevin had any particular training for a collaborative ministry, they are learning. They clearly realize that they cannot work as Lone Rangers at Trinity. Rather, they must complement each other, share ministry, coordinate their work and schedules, and lead the rest of the staff to function as a team. To learn how to function as colleagues, they have decided to meet weekly to discuss their mutual ministry at Trinity. Further, to learn how to function as a team, the entire staff is planning to have a retreat and bring in an outside leader from time to time.

As Roy Oswald points out, the key to the success of the large church is "the multiple staff and its ability to manage the diversity of its ministries in a collegial manner."[12] When staffs fail to work cooperatively, it drains the energy required to coordinate and plan the ongoing ministry of the church. Yet far too many large churches find their staffs crippled, even immobilized by staff conflicts.

The lesson is clear: those planning to serve in multiple staff ministry in any capacity would do well to evaluate their ability to work collaboratively. They should also seek to discover whether the staff where they intend to serve can work together.

Observe further that in describing Trinity I have quite liberally used words like program, mission statement, goals and objectives, administration, collegiality, and coordination. And no wonder. Such words accurately describe the ethos of the large church. Pastors and associates who are not comfortable with those dynamics would probably serve more faithfully and effectively in a small or medium-sized church. Other contexts would more fully maximize their direct interpersonal and pastoral care skills.

Not only will you need to be aware of the dynamics of your church, you must also get started with your judicatory. Will it not be important to understand the various cultural lifestyles of your community and your congregation? Let's now probe what a proper start-up with your community and your judicatory might look like.

CHAPTER 4

TESTING THE WATERS BEYOND YOUR CONGREGATION

S tan, who was moving into his second pastorate, had already told our New Pastorate Start-up Seminar that he was interested in putting down deep roots in his community. Recall that he had not taken time to do so in his first pastorate.

"Before you begin," said Heather, "I hope you'll also help us learn how to get started with our denominations. I'm really afraid I won't know what to do when I finally become ordained!"

"I hope we can address both of your concerns because they are crucial in beginning any new pastorate," I replied. "Let's begin with your question, Heather."

Learning Your Judicatory

Most readers belong to a presbytery, conference, association, diocese, or other judicatory. That judicatory was involved in your journey toward ordination; it will be involved in your daily practice of ministry. You operate within the parameters of your judicatory as described and prescribed (and proscribed!) by the polity of your denomination. Unless you belong to an independent church, a certain denomination has supervised or licensed or ordained you; therefore you must work within its guidelines. For a vital, ongoing ministry all clergy need continuing support, fellowship, inspiration, guidance, and correction. Thus you need to know your judicatory!

Clergy, however, sometimes complain about their judicatories, especially about long, boring, and inefficient meetings. Our colleagues also anger us by the decisions they make, although we pay lip service to the principle that our sisters and brothers are more likely to discern the will of Christ *acting together* than we are acting individually or even in our own congregations. And we may resent the power that some officials seem to exercise over our careers.

Sooner or later every judicatory stretches our belief in the system to the limit. We are all fallible, sinful human beings seeking to serve Christ. Thus the systems, the judicatories we form, are flawed. But they are the only systems we have, and we dare to believe that Christ still rules the church by Word and Spirit.

To work faithfully and effectively, then, establish a relationship with your judicatory. The following suggestions, adapted from material prepared by the United Church of Christ, will vary from denomination to denomination.[1] Pick and choose from this cafeteria line whatever menu items best fit your situation.

Visit your judicatory office. Though it may not be located in your immediate area (particularly if you are serving in Alaska or Texas!), when an opportunity arises visit your regional headquarters.

- Meet the judicatory staff. Ask them what advice they have to give you as you begin your ministry.
- Make sure they put you on their mailing list.
- Inquire about any orientation events the judicatory has scheduled.
- Get to know the support staff so they will recognize you when you call the office later.
- Understand the structure of your judicatory; printed materials may be available.

Most judicatories help you with these entry procedures. Sometimes, however, you have to take the initiative yourself to become informed.

Get involved.
- Attend judicatory meetings. Maintaining your denominational membership probably requires your attendance anyway.
- Participate in continuing education events sponsored by the judicatory.

- Serve on committees and task forces as opportunities arise. While at first you may feel you are being asked to serve in the more menial roles, take those jobs and do them well. Remember that Jesus said, "But I am among you as one who serves" (Luke 22:27). So should we be among people as those who serve. You can imbue every so-called "menial" opportunity with your own creativity and efficiency.

Communicate.

- Receive and read judicatory mailings. Later you will be able to decide what you can safely discard!
- Put judicatory officials on your church mailing list. ✗
- Inform judicatory staff of events and activities in your congregation. Seek their advice in planning those events.
- Annually notify the proper committee in your judicatory of your status, if required.
- Be supportive of fellow pastors and churches in your judicatory and show your willingness to work with them.

Participate in your judicatory's orientation program. When you move to a new pastorate, sign up for whatever briefing is offered. You will not only feel more at home within your structures but will begin to build working relationships with other clergy.

Additionally, if you are beginning your ministry, take part in a New Pastor Support Group. Fundamental questions about ministry will rapidly surface. Sometimes judicatories provide ongoing support groups to help you answer those questions. At their best such training programs establish a context in which you can reflect upon your experiences in ministry, share your joys and pains, refine your skills, deepen your spirituality, and give yourself a chance to relax. While not perfect, denominational attempts to aid new pastors as their careers unfold are well worth the time and money invested in them. They can mean the difference between a growing ministry and a shattered career.

Discovering Your Community

The salesman in *The Music Man* said, "You gotta know the territory." And certain ministers should know their territory.

How easy it is to forget that every church is set in a specific context. Therefore what works in one area will not necessarily work in another. Before you can ever minister effectively you need to learn the culture of your area—its norms, its lifestyles, its values, its speech, its power brokers, its hidden side. More than one minister has stumbled badly by not taking time to understand the nature of his or her church community! A humorous example explains why.

John, a seminary student, was serving as a summer intern in a very conservative church in Alabama. The monthly session (or church board) meeting was in full swing. The pastor had invited the young intern to sit with him and five elders, all of whom had been on the session over twenty years.

The meeting moved from topic to topic until the elders finally considered how they could motivate more people to participate in church events other than through their ice cream socials. They were searching for that one new way that would bring people flocking to the doors of the church. When the conversation became quiet, John thought to himself: "Now is the time to make my move and offer the suggestion of a lifetime." So he raised his hand to speak.

The pastor called on him, saying, "John, we value your input because you have trained in seminary and studied new ways of doing old things. I'm sure what you have to say will benefit us."

"Mr. Moderator, and members of the session," John said deliberately, "I think it's time for this church to consider having a wine and cheese party. It's a sure way to bring adults together in a culturally enriching way."

The silence was deafening. Mouths dropped open. Eyes popped out of heads. The intern didn't know he had made his suggestion of a lifetime in a very conservative church that had never even served wine instead of grape juice in communion services. Further, the church was located in a *dry county*. You "gotta know the territory" indeed!

So how do you start learning the territory? Begin by learning this principle: *Your congregation is an open system.* In other words, it has permeable boundaries so that there is a flow between the environment and the congregation. The congregation is always adjusting to what is going on in the environment.[2]

Still, an open system implies that the congregation interacts with its environment. Any congregation can respond and make choices that affect its destiny. It can challenge and even transcend the powerful determining influence of its context and influence it instead. For in their social and faith traditions all congregations embody "ideas and inspiration, beliefs and experience" that enable them to confront and rise above their context.[3] No one would contend that this is easy or that it happens very often, but a congregation is not completely determined by its social context. Does not the church, despite its imperfect nature, march to the beat of a different drummer?

How do you learn the territory—the church's context—more specifically? *At the most fundamental level, become involved in your community.* A clergy couple, Beth and Brent, describe how they became involved: "We joined civic organizations. We went to dance recitals, Little League games, community basketball games. We did these things because we genuinely wanted to, but, looking back, we were doing more than just passing the time. We were learning the context of the church—what was and is important to our members outside their lives in the church. We were showing our congregation that we cared about them at all times and places, not just in the church on Sunday morning. We also gave them something to be proud of in the community; they were glad to be able to claim us as their ministers in community contexts. Those kinds of things went a long way toward helping build the church's self-esteem."[4]

Yet Beth and Brent were also learning how their church and context interacted. Said Brent, "I also coached basketball. What one has to be careful about is getting into Sunday games. I think that if one is involved with sports, there could be the chance to influence policy regarding the scheduling of games. But exercise great caution, for children's sports constitutes a powerful religion."[5]

Brent indicated that he knew his church could influence its environment by challenging the scheduling of sports on Sundays. His congregation, demonstrating a previous observation, contained social and faith traditions that could enable it to challenge and transcend their environment. Brent also knew the strong grip the environment held on families because of sports. Thus the congregation might pay a price for confronting its culture over the issue.

Further, by becoming involved in their community, Brent and Beth were discovering how to minister to their people. As they grasped community values, lifestyles, and basic needs, they could then relate the gospel to their community through their preaching, teaching, caregiving, and programming. For example, if excessive sports competition was harming children, Brent and Beth could work with both parents and children in Sunday school classes to lessen its destructive effects.

More formal tools for community analysis are available for Beth and Brent to use. Among many choices, the "Hallett model" is appealing, for it can offer an eye-opening probe.[5] For maximum benefit, it requires, as Roy Oswald points out, an ongoing support group composed of persons from the political, economic, legal, voluntary, and media sectors. If Brent and Beth so choose, they can meet with such persons, asking them questions like, "Where are the places in which the most human suffering seems to occur?" and "What are the key social/political/economic issues that need attention in this community?"[6] A group like that can furnish invaluable assistance to this clergy couple as they get started in their new pastorate.

Short of engaging in a full-blown mission study, Beth and Brent can draw a series of mental or written maps as they go about their work. Carl Dudley has said that pastors and church leaders carry seven maps in their heads.[7] Taken as a whole, the maps provide a helpful way for new pastors to understand their context.

1. *The membership map.* As you gradually learn your community, you will note where your members live and be able to tell a story about each family or describe an event that happened there.

2. *The evangelism map.* This can be an actual map, kept in the church office, depicting prospects, and maintained by a few key people.

3. *Physical boundaries map.* Your church building is located in a geographic area that has a name and has boundaries that others recognize.

4. *Populations and lifestyles map.* People talk about changes taking place on particular neighborhood blocks, and also the characteristics of the people who live there. For more information on how to use census data, see *Marketing for Congregations.*[8]

5. *Traffic flow and centers of community map.* Slowly you can build an in-depth knowledge of major and minor streets, shopping malls, schools, libraries, and other churches.

6. *Major institutions map.* You discover the major employers, educational institutions, hospitals, military bases, and prisons. These institutions form the social, political, and economic anchors in the community.

7. *Power brokers and decision makers map.* They constitute part of the shadow government of community life that is both formal and informal. They keep the community going more than most people realize.

You can segment the seven maps, of course. If you are mainly interested in being a pastor to your church members, the membership map will suffice. Or, if you are primarily interested in the important work of evangelism, the evangelism map will suffice. To minister holistically, you need to develop all seven maps and keep them in your head. They will help you both to understand and relate the gospel to your community.

As you build your mental maps, you will record much useful data. You will remember a conversation you heard between two bankers who asserted that nothing is ever done at City Council unless the council members consult Bill Wilson, the retired CEO of the local mill. That growing body of knowledge will directly influence your preaching, your program recommendations, and how you go about working in the community.

On a long-term basis, the mission study committee of middle-sized and large churches needs to do an in-depth analysis of the community to determine where there are hurts and needs to which the church should respond. Such a study will yield even more long-term benefits to a congregation because leaders *and* members—not just the pastor—will generate the knowledge and act on it. Moreover, it will further lay the groundwork for equipping the members for the work of ministry.[9]

Exploring Cultural Lifestyles

For too long theological education has assumed that "one size fits all." That is, we have acted as though graduates could take one kind of educational experience and apply it equally to all people elsewhere, regardless of their lifestyles. That simply will not work, as Tex Sample has identified that there are essentially three U.S. lifestyles, the cultural left, right, and middle.[10] Competent ministry requires pastors to learn the lifestyles of their community. And when they do, they may have to unlearn part of what they have learned in their theological education.

The cultural left. This large group of Americans consists of baby boomers who seek self-fulfillment while being inner-directed; another group who seeks immediate, vital experience, including the mystical; and a final group of socially conscious Americans who often use "single-issue politics" in a confrontational style. The "New Agers" are found among all the groups on the cultural left, but also in the cultural middle.

If you are beginning a new pastorate, discover whether your congregation has a cultural left. Seminary education will have furnished some methods for reaching the baby boomers on the left. Large churches—and to a lesser extent the medium-sized church—can offer option-filled programs and alternative approaches that attract more people on the cultural left. These programs provide marvelous opportunities to capitalize on the boomer's mystical therapeutic interests, their hopes of combining spirituality and social transformation, and their hunger for relationships. For example, Jonathan and Elizabeth, who typify the cultural left, might be excited by a church offering a seven-week program on holistic spirituality. Through the program, which teaches Christian techniques of meditation, they would not only learn ways to grow in their personal faith, but also how to put their faith into action in the community.

Offering a wide array of programs to meet the boomers' needs doesn't mean the church has to embrace their lifestyle. However, it does require that the church be willing to meet them where they are. Perhaps in so doing both the church and the boomers will develop a mutual appreciation of contrasting lifestyles.

The cultural right. The cultural right is a difficult group to categorize because of its diversity in income, politics, and background. Therefore it would be grossly unfair to stereotype the group in terms of any one class.

The first group includes a significant number of blue-collar people who long to be respectable and who emphasize the family, traditional values, and love for country. Also within the cultural right, which prizes individualism and self-reliance, one may discover a wide diversity ranging from wealthy backers of conservative political candidates to hard-living, politically alienated persons who feel left out of society. The cultural right further includes some poor and near poor, who tend to be uneducated and elderly.

Because of your own background and theological training, you might find it easy or difficult to minister to the cultural right. If difficult, learn to appreciate the right in order to speak to it. For example, to study in seminary that it's idolatrous to *worship* the nation is both biblical and helpful. For God alone is God and worthy of our worship. Yet is it not also wise to begin where the cultural right is in its love for the nation? Certainly we clergy also love our nation, even though we know that it imperfectly offers "liberty and justice for all." So when we criticize our nation, we must do so as those who have a lover's quarrel with it. Thus, if you are working with the cultural right, identify *first* the system of meaning. That's how you earn the right to be heard on other issues.

As another illustration, let every expression of a folksy theology from people be your invitation to listen, to understand, and to identify with people in their viewpoint. A theology that often stresses a God who is active even in securing parking places might be a personal attempt to deal with one's own sense of powerlessness. When you penetrate someone's frame of reference, you reveal yourself as a fellow journeyer, not as a judge.

Again, you may be a "think and do" Christian, not a "believe and feel" Christian, as are many people on the right. If so, you will be pushed to rethink the way you preach, teach, conduct meetings, give personal care, and lead worship. In the process you may well come not only to appreciate the cultural right but also to celebrate their core faith with them.

The cultural middle. Into tight focus now come the professional and business people who form the backbone of many mainline churches. These often successful people are upper middle class, gifted, hardworking, and achievement-oriented.

A subgroup within the successful, however, is only striving to make it to the top and be like those who have made it. Holding far fewer professional and technical jobs, "they overspend and are typically in debt."[11] Others who are lumped into the successful category can rightly be judged as conflicted. They are trapped between commitment to their careers and fidelity to their families.

To minister to people in the cultural middle, note certain characteristics they possess. A key quality is their stress on individualism. Such individualism leads them to be lonely and to believe only in individual effort. They may not be concerned, for example, about addressing societal injustices, but merely what individuals can do acting alone. Isn't that to be expected since they constitute the ranks of privilege and want to protect their position?

If you are ministering in a congregation of this type, your pastoral leadership is badly needed. You can help shape the congregation's commitment to social justice and the issues of our day.

Another place for pastoral leadership is in the midst of the painful experiences that tear at the cultural middle. Many suffer from wrenching stress. Others struggle for dignity through achievement, while still others are haunted by failure or even the fear of failure. Moreover, because of the pressure to succeed, many parents—especially fathers—fail to anchor their families as they should. Thus they live with gnawing regret. The church can challenge the dominant ethos of this group and enable it to embrace a new worldview.

A further task for you as pastor with the cultural middle is in your approach to theology. Since people in the cultural middle come from business and professional settings in which it is customary to explain everything, they demand the same in the church. So, as pastor of the cultural middle, you engage in explanatory theology, as Sample calls it.[12] By using this approach you lay bare the pain of life that afflicts the cultural middle and show how God's grace brings healing balm. To those caught in a maddening competitive struggle to put themselves over with their good works, you explain what they are doing and what inevitably happens. But always you proclaim the good news of God's grace, which if accepted, can bring an end to their anxious striving.

Yet another place to employ explanatory theology is in the small group life of the church. Numerous business and professional people are reluctant to expose the raw edges of their pain. But their reluctance can be overcome in a communal atmosphere of trust and acceptance. There they will be more likely to peel off the layers of veneer covering their successful exteriors and reveal the pain that surely throbs in their hearts. In such an atmosphere they can more readily see themselves as they are and perhaps become more willing to engage in the church's mission to the outside world.

So your start-up in a new pastorate requires you to know the predominant lifestyles of your community and congregation. If you don't understand the community, you cannot serve them effectively. Remember: "You gotta know the territory!"

Yet, not to be overlooked in the important work of discovering context and congregation is the task of dealing with the conflict that inevitably comes to the surface. For as we interact with our congregations and community groups, we encounter conflict in all of its multiple facets. Does not conflict management become a crucial skill for starting up wisely and well? The following chapter explores that need.

CHAPTER 5

DEALING WITH CONFLICT

For a discussion starter, I asked the seminar participants what came to mind when they heard the word "conflict." I wrote their answers on the board as they rapidly called out: "Fighting, anger, tension, trouble, hurt . . . " Only after the initial flow of negative images did more positive images like "creativity, growth, and harmony" emerge.

When I next asked them what they expected to learn about managing conflict, several replied, "We think you're going to teach us how to put a lid on it!"

Again, upon administering an inventory that measures conflict management styles, I discovered that *avoiding* conflict was their most prevalent style.[1]

Put these three exercises together, and what picture do you get? Essentially a picture of the negativity of conflict and that it should be controlled and/or avoided.

If that sums up your basic attitude toward conflict as you begin a new pastorate, pay close attention to this chapter. For maintaining a negative attitude toward conflict will produce only negative experiences with it. Putting a lid on all conflict in the church is difficult, if not impossible—and certainly not desirable. Moreover, avoiding conflict will not make it go away; it will usually build up until it sometimes breaks out with frightening intensity. Would it not be better to learn how to face it and work creatively in the midst of it?

Yet you may scarcely be able to imagine disastrous conflict erupting in your ministry. But someday the proverbial honeymoon you enjoy at the beginning of most pastorates will come to an end. I do not know what will bring about its demise, but you will be rocked—count on it.

Your phone may ring as mine did one Sunday afternoon just when I was thoroughly exhausted from a busy morning. "Bob, would you meet me at the church this afternoon?" a church elder inquired. "There's something I want to talk with you about."

Though I agreed to meet with him, I knew I was in trouble. I was not mistaken, for the elder proceeded to tell me everything he thought I was doing wrong in my ministry. He even mentioned that I was not stopping by his home and having a cup of coffee as the previous minister had done. The fact that we had 1,200 members in the church apparently made no difference to him. After the encounter, I felt battered—my honeymoon was definitely over!

Now, conflict in one's first pastorate is especially bothersome. But it's also troubling whenever it appears, whether it is in your first pastorate or fifth. For no matter how much theory you know or previous experience you have had in the church, conflict will take on a different dimension for you as a pastor. Suddenly you realize that more is at stake than you had thought; in fact, it may seem like a life and death matter. Your career itself could be in jeopardy, particularly if the conflict revolves around *you* as pastor. That possibility was not in your wildest fantasies when you became a minister!

At first you will become aware of your own *internal* conflict as you engage in ministry. No doubt you will move into a pastorate with high ideals about what a church should be and do. You believe, for example, that the church should reach out to evangelize and serve its community and the world. But you are often jarred when you realize that many of your members don't share that ideal. Every time you move to another pastorate you hope and pray it will be different.

Once, when consulting with a church served by a new seminary graduate, I met with the Long Range Planning Committee. After the meeting George, the pastor, drew me aside and said, "I became aware tonight that most of these people would be comfortable just coming to worship, enjoying fellowship dinners, but then doing nothing else. That's painful for me to realize." George's intense internal conflict was obvious.

You will also soon become aware of *external* conflict. While you will be involved in all conflict—people cannot perceive you as neutral—much of it will not be your own doing. You will come to know the battles various members have fought and are now fighting, how families have lined up on one side or the other of sundry issues, and how certain persons have always been thorns in the flesh of every minister who ever served that church.

When you first encounter conflict, you will come up dripping with perspiration and seek all the help you can get. Be assured, nonetheless, that even your best attempts to deal creatively with conflict won't always yield positive results. In fact, you will frequently fail. At other times all you will be able to do is to keep matters civil among your members. Yet, achieving even a cease-fire might be a victory, far superior to the divisive explosions that leave church people broken, bruised, and scarred for life. Further, there may be times when you become so embroiled in the conflict itself that an outside consultant will be needed. To prepare yourself for the conflict that will surely shatter your tranquility, let's look at conflict from several different standpoints.

A Biblical Understanding

Studying what the Bible says about conflict will change your view that you should always avoid conflict.

That doesn't mean you will be able to avoid it, only that as an ideal you often need to face it. The Bible is saturated with conflict from Genesis to Revelation, from Cain and Abel to the final great battle of Armageddon. In between you discover a myriad of other conflicts. These can sometimes be *intrapersonal* as in the battles the tragic Saul fought within himself, or *interpersonal* as between David and Saul, or sometimes *intrafamilial* as between Jacob and Esau. They may also be *intragroup* as between the Northern and Southern kingdoms, or *intergroup* as between the children of Israel and the Philistines, or *substantive* as in the council meeting in Jerusalem when the early Christians were trying to decide whether or not to admit Gentiles into the infant church without forcing them to conform to the customs of Moses.

The entire biblical drama, of course, focuses on the overarching conflict between good and evil. Sometimes the Bible depicts the struggle as a battle between light and darkness, as did John: "The light shines in the darkness, and the darkness did not overcome it" (John 1:5). At other times the Bible depicts the kind of internal struggle that paralyzed Paul: "For I do not do the good I want, but the evil I do not want is what I do" (Rom. 7:19). The Bible declares, moreover, that God provided the way for humankind to win the victory over sin and evil through Jesus Christ. The Bible further describes how humankind resisted God's plan of salvation so often, preferring the shadows of darkness to the bright light of Christ. From a biblical perspective, therefore, the Christian life is certainly not for the fainthearted.

Then as now conflict was integral to life. Whenever the gospel of the kingdom is proclaimed, the world opposes it. For the kingdom seeks to deliver a death blow to unjustice, to right every wrong, and to oppose any power that would dehumanize us. Doesn't conflict thus become inevitable for Christians? For ministers? It could hardly be otherwise—the biblical narrative makes this point plainly.

A Theological Understanding

As we further explore the nature of conflict theologically, we draw certain conclusions. First, it's not wrong to have *differences* in the church, for we are different human beings, who possess different personalities, who were reared in different homes, and who were molded by different cultural influences. Would we not therefore be surprised *not* to have differences?

It is not wrong to state our differences and assert our viewpoint. Notice I said *assert* our viewpoint, not *overpower* others. We can declare and contend forcefully for what we believe without overpowering others. How? By giving others the same freedom we give ourselves. By listening to them and seeking to understand as we would be understood.

Our third conclusion is this: given the conditions of our finite existence and our sinful nature, conflict is potentially destructive and debilitating.[2] Moreover, in all human conflict there is probably an element of the sinful misuse of freedom and self-assertion at the expense of the real good. After all, we are conditioned to win. Is it not difficult to consider someone else's viewpoint as sympathetically as we do our own?

Under such conditions, then, it is doubtful that conflict can be resolved without sin putting in an appearance, if ever so slightly. Whether you agree or not, the point should be clear that conflict has at least the potential to be destructive and tinged with sin, just as it can be constructive and promote the common good.

There's more. Even if you think it's possible to resolve disputes without sin being a factor, you will probably agree that conflict definitely has its dangers, its downside. In other words, it's never risk-free. Though you initiate an action you think nobody *could* oppose, you may be astounded to see opposition develop nevertheless. A minister once took the initiative to move the pulpit in his church about one yard from its old position and touched off an intense controversy. That incident occurred in a church that had just raised one million dollars to help the poor! One never knows what action will spark a battle.

Theologically, what is the *goal* of conflict? Conflict is not an end in itself. We don't express our viewpoints on issues merely to foster disputes, as though creating conflicts were our primary goal. No, the conflict is only a means, a process to obtain other ends, other goals. We state what we believe is the best way to expand church facilities, knowing that others will differ with us. Yet our goal is to expand our church facilities, not to create conflict. The resulting conflict becomes part of the process to achieve that goal.

In many of our conflicts, does not *reconciliation* become our goal? For people can get polarized on the best way to expand the church facilities. Our goals, then, in the resulting conflict are twofold: first, reconciliation, because we work to enable warring factions to live in peace and harmony; and second, to decide how best to expand the church facilities.

But, as Speed Leas makes clear, reconciliation is not a result we can produce. Rather, it is a gift of God's grace. All we can do is to create an environment in which reconciliation is more likely to occur.

Sometimes, however, our goal will be less lofty, more proximate. In those cases we may establish ground rules for discussing issues, such as requiring persons to restate the previous speaker's position before stating their own. We thereby enable persons to listen to one another so that the ultimate goal of reconciliation can happen.

Nonetheless, perhaps there is an even larger vision of what Christians are seeking to create in conflict. That vision is *shalom.* Though we ordinarily translate shalom as peace, Jack L. Stotts says its "core meaning is that of wholeness, health, and security." Such wholeness, health, and security does "not mean individual tranquility in the midst of external turbulence." Nor does it mean peace of mind, in which we "escape from the frustrations and care of the surrounding environment." Rather, we work to establish a society in which God, humans, and nature are in communion; in other words, where fulfillment exists for all creation. That social state is shalom.[4]

Surely, God's shalom is a worthy goal to work toward in church conflicts. When starting up in a new pastorate, let this vision of God's wholeness, health, and security for all guide you if conflict arises. This ultimate vision will lead you to set up processes in which people can move toward shalom for all creation.

A Systemic Understanding

In addition to biblical and theological insights, modern systems theory is amazingly applicable to church conflicts. The more you understand systems theory, the better you will understand church conflicts.

"Any group of human beings in regular contact with each other is a system," says Kenneth Mitchell.[5] When human beings work together, live together, or interact with one another over a period of time, they develop certain patterns of interacting. This concept applies to families, churches, businesses, and communities. Each such system is composed of persons who expect certain kinds of behavior, try to get their own needs met, attempt to carry out group purposes, and develop ways to preserve the group. As Mitchell makes clear, "Systems behave as though they were persons with lives of their own."[6]

For example, systems resist change just as people do. It makes no difference whether the proffered change is good or bad, a system resists it.[7] So regardless of how good and logical your proposals seem to you, others will resist them. Why? Because of *homeostasis*, from the Greek meaning "to stay the same." Systems go to remarkable extremes to keep everything the same.

Suppose, for example, in your church Tom has always spoken in favor of giving ten percent of the church budget to benevolent causes before the needs of the local church are considered. But Tom suddenly dies. Strangely, Dave pops up to voice Tom's same concerns about giving to benevolent causes first. Dave thus moves into and assumes the role Tom had occupied before he died. So systems try to stay the same whether proposals are constructive, as in this case, or negative.

Actually, this systemic phenomenon can be frightening, particularly if you plan to move to a "problem church." You may think that you can easily provide the kind of leadership a problem church needs, only to find out soon that the system is deeply troubled. Problem churches "run off" minister after minister. Though change for such churches is possible, it's never easy.

When things suddenly go haywire in your church for no apparent reason, ask key questions like, "Why now? What has gone out of balance?"[8] Edwin Friedman says that the issues that are being disputed are not the real issues. Thus we ask whether there have been significant changes in the emotional system, either in the families of key leaders or within the congregation itself. A change in the personal life of a church leader could prompt a conflict or the sudden resignation of a key staff person. In a church I served, I was puzzled by how upset several people were when the financial secretary resigned. On the defensive, I felt compelled to go into lengthy explanations. Now I see that homeostatic forces were at work. The secretary's resignation upset the system people had grown used to in the church.

Here the concept of the "emotional triangle" will prove immensely helpful. Murray Bowen has posited that *triangles* are the basic building blocks of systems.[9] The theory is that all groups of two persons are inherently unstable and seek a third element to stabilize the relationship. The third element may be a physical object, a person, an issue, one's job, a hobby, or a number of other things.

To illustrate, a husband and wife who are troubled beneath the surface of their marriage may focus on their daughter's problems in an attempt to stabilize their own relationship. The third person who is caught in the middle—the daughter in the above case—is said to be "triangled." As long as the husband and wife stay focused on their daughter's problems, they treat each other decently. But whenever they attempt to relate to each other, their old animosity returns.

Parishioners often triangle ministers to stabilize relationships in their own families and jobs. When you suspect you are being triangled, it's helpful to ask, "What's going on here?" A parishioner whose son apparently committed suicide—it could not be proved, however—was always needling me about something in my ministry. Was he triangling me in an attempt to stabilize his relationship with his departed son?

Another phenomenon that readily demonstrates the systemic nature of churches is *interconnectedness*. You can't move one end of a seesaw without moving the other end also. By the same token, one change, even though it seems minor, will produce many other changes.

An example. A church observed that children from a minority group had begun using the church playground for kickball after school. When church members objected, the board voted to put a fence around the playground and to padlock it. But then mysterious acts of vandalism began to occur—broken windows, trash on the grounds, and spray paint on the church walls. Those acts of vandalism in turn scared some of the members so much that they refused to attend night meetings at the church. Did the children, deprived of their playground, commit the vandalism? It was never known for sure, only suspected. Systems are interconnected, and changes introduced in one part produce ripple effects throughout. Every action produces consequences, though we persist in thinking it is isolated and self-contained.

A Personal Understanding

Work on your personal attitude toward conflict and how you usually behave in conflictive situations. You may discover that you are deathly afraid of conflict. You may also see that you can't face conflict, no matter how hard you try—avoidance is too deeply rooted in your personhood. If you can't face it, you may need to obtain counseling about this issue to help you find out what is blocking you, what keeps you afraid, and how you can break free.

When you begin a new pastorate, take Speed Leas's inventory on styles of managing church conflict.[10] Your style can range all the way from *avoiding* conflict to *controlling* it tightly. Then a year later retake the inventory to see whether you note any differences emerging in your style or styles.

Be aware of your feelings, thoughts, and behavior in conflictive situations. What happens to you when a domineering man challenges you at a board meeting on a recommendation you have proposed? Do you tense up, back down at once, or listen to what he has to say? At a deep level, what does your "gut theology," as Hugh Halverstadt calls it, tell you?[11] He describes gut theologies as feeling-based ideas about conflict acquired from our experiences between birth and ten years of age. We later learned

Christian teachings and adapted them to fit our childhood assumptions about conflict. As we mature, however, we can reassess feeling-based thoughts from our early years and decide if they are appropriate.

Attempt to practice new behaviors. If you have diligently evaded asking a leader what she meant by her remark at the church door last Sunday, resolve now to ask her. You may be able to do so, then again you may find yourself retreating fearfully.

By all means, don't withdraw from people you are hostile toward, at least not automatically. Rather, consider moving toward them. As long as you keep backing away, your hostility and alienation will only increase.

Model an ability to handle conflict and utilize it. Edwin Friedman's suggestion to maintain what he calls a "non-anxious presence" is instructive. He refers to the capacity of "clergy to contain their own anxiety regarding congregational matters, both those not related to them, as well as those where they become the identified focus."[12] When you contain your anxiety, you reduce anxiety throughout the congregation. If you react anxiously to threatening situations, you feed your anxiety back into the congregation.

Yet in each of the above situations, your own personal attitude, conditioned by your gut theology, will be the controlling factor. You may identify with Paul, who cried out, "For I do not do the good I want . . . " (Rom. 7:19). All these recommendations rest on the premise that conflict needs to be faced and can be good. That never guarantees that you will face it, however. So, become a diligent student of how you are personally handling conflict.

A Congregational Understanding

When talking with leaders and members after you go to a church, ask them how the congregation has handled conflict in the past. If they continually say, "We haven't had any conflicts in our church," be very suspicious. It is wise to assume that diversity is present in every group. Lurking beneath the surface of seemingly homogeneous churches are differences of opinion about goals, methods, values, and theology. Will you allow those differences to appear or keep them buried? If they emerge, then the group can deal with them constructively. If they stay buried, the group will appear to be harmonious but lack the deep unity that is derived from a mutual appreciation of differences.

Dealing with Conflict

Use this w/
PPR + AM comm.

One plan I have followed in dozens of groups and classes is to provide them with an instrument that helps them analyze how well we have been working together. (See Appendix 1.) Even when I have thought things were going well, someone has said, "I don't feel a part of the group," or "I don't feel we are using our time wisely." How could I have misread the group? *Because people tend to suppress conflict, especially in the church.* Only by giving them a chance to write down their internal responses in a non-threatening atmosphere are they likely to speak out. Diversity is always present. The question is, "Will we allow it to rise to the surface?"

Sometimes you may even find it necessary to *stimulate* conflict. When? If leaders and members refuse to face the reality of their situation. Suppose they won't face the fact that the church is declining numerically and financially. Then calmly present some graphs covering the last five years. That might enable them to see the true picture.

Teach conflict management whenever possible. At retreats with church leaders and members, deal with this theme. Go over the material in this chapter. Give people a chance to assess their conflict management styles and to review strategies for dealing with conflict. Lead them in a Bible study such as Acts 15, the council meeting in Jerusalem.

In your preaching deal with church conflict, though not necessarily when you are in the middle of one! Use biblical texts like Acts 15 just mentioned or a wealth of texts provided by William H. Willimon in his book *Preaching About Conflict in the Local Church.*[13]

By using these suggestions, you may become a better conflict manager. But don't be surprised if you conclude that you need to work on your skills much more. A minister once said to me, "I've been to several conflict management workshops but I still don't manage conflict well." It is a complex area of ministry; in fact, managing conflict may be the quintessential administrative skill ministers need.

In a sense we have already anticipated the next chapter which deals with change. Much conflict results from change, as we have seen. Does that mean we dare not initiate change? No, but certain principles and strategies, if followed, will more probably ensure successful change. We look at those principles and strategies next.

CHAPTER 6

EFFECTING CHANGE

D o you recall George's intense discomfort over the apparent complacency of his congregation?

"Don't lose that discomfort," I told him, "for God put it there. But the situation is by no means hopeless. Start with the people where they are. Plan changes with them. You've got some good people to work with here."

Taking heart, George replied, "Well, I have thought about meeting with some of the leaders you met tonight and asking them if they felt the same discomfort I feel."

"Good idea," I said. "Work with them, plan with them, and gradually move together to where you think God wants you to be as a church. It won't happen all at once, but change can happen."

(Yet nothing is more maddening to pastors than what appears to be stubbornness on the part of their churches to be and do what the gospel requires.)Seminary graduates in particular are bothered by this stubbornness. Eager to put new ideas and programs into action, they often charge into their first parishes and then completely ignore the dynamics of change. Even before they try to understand their new situation, they want to change everything.

Example A: A new pastor goes to his first church, a small church located in a rural area. The first Sunday he notices that the pianist is playing the hymns much too slowly for his taste. The second Sunday produces the same result, as does the third. Thoroughly frustrated, the pastor says to her, "Your playing is unacceptable. I'm going to ask someone else to play from now on." But the pianist just happens to be the granddaughter of the church patriarch! Predictably, an intense controversy erupts.

Example B: A young pastor goes to her first church, a small church of about 100 members. She is convinced that the Lord's Supper should be observed more often than once a quarter. She therefore studies the issue with her Worship Committee, which decides to recommend to the governing board that the church observe the sacrament monthly instead of quarterly. The pastor is confident the recommendation will pass. However, after the committee makes its recommendation to the board, the church patriarch says, "Well, I'm afraid the Lord's Supper wouldn't mean as much to me if we observed it every month. When it's observed once a quarter, it's special." The recommendation of the committee is killed by an overwhelming vote.

Nor are more seasoned pastors immune to the disease of trying to change a church all at once without understanding either its context or the dynamics of change.

Example C: A pastor who had dedicated his ministry to churches in small towns becomes pastor of yet another small-town church of 125 members. In his previous church he had become active in community voter registration. His unusually progressive board, while not active in the cause, nonetheless supported and defended him whenever he was criticized by church members or the community. The third week he is in his new church, he decides to participate in a voter registration drive. Some of the church leaders hear about it and react with disfavor. Soon they begin to criticize him for almost everything he does, even minor decisions like when he keeps office hours. Though it's never stated, he suspects the deeper issue lies in his participation in the voter registration drive. Six months later he is asked to resign and look for another church.

Example D: A new associate pastor becomes concerned when she discovers in her second pastorate that the hymns sung in the Sunday service do not use inclusive language. When she announces the hymns, therefore, she tells the congregation to change the word "man" to "us" and to insert "God" for every male pronoun used to refer to God. Members begin complaining about her "performance" to the head of staff. Two write letters to the church board requesting that she stop changing the hymns they have been singing from their hymnbook for the last twenty-five years.

Few who read this book will disagree with the desire of the four pastors to effect change. After all, their goals are commendable. They wanted better church music, more frequent communion services, total community voter registration, and more inclusive language in worship services. Nor would anyone contend that they lacked the courage of their convictions. Yet many would question their judgment about the timing of their actions and their awareness of change dynamics.

As we have seen, *all systems resist change.* The well-known "Seven Last Words of the Church" remain alive and well in every church I have seen: "We've never done it that way before." And churches particularly resist change if they have had no part in planning the changes that will affect them. In each of the previous mini-cases, except one, the new pastors ignored this basic principle.

Mistakes Pastors Often Make When They Move

Here's a rundown of the mistakes pastors most frequently make in regard to change in their new pastorates. We track them quickly now, but will return to them later when considering strategies for change.

—feeling they have the truth and must straighten out the "poor, misguided souls" in their churches. Were not they themselves nurtured in the faith by the "poor, misguided souls" of some church?
—being driven compulsively to turn things upside down in their churches. The message they communicate to the congregation is: "The pastor thinks we're doing everything wrong."
—forgetting to affirm the congregation for all they see the congregation doing well. In the absence of the pastor's affirmation, leaders will occasionally resign, thinking they have not done a good job.
—failing to recognize that the dynamics of change in the small church are different from the large church. Change can occur in small churches but is especially alarming because they don't want be in the vanguard of anything.

—choosing to fight the wrong battles. Many issues for which they seem to be willing to put their careers on the line have little to do with the gospel.

—attempting to effect change too soon without building a relationship of trust with the congregation, particularly with its leaders. They forget that they have to earn the trust and confidence of their people.

—not putting themselves in the shoes of their parishioners to see life as they see it. Instead, they assume that their university and seminary background has given them the correct lenses through which to view life.

—preferring to adopt the role of the lonely prophet rather than training the congregation to see the prophetic implications of the gospel. Is not ministry given to the whole people of God?

—rushing to start a program they have seen work well somewhere else. But they don't first judge the potential fit between the program and the people they are *now* serving.

—using the same leadership style they practiced elsewhere without considering the needs of their new congregation. If they were more controlling leaders in one congregation, they automatically employ that same controlling style in their next pastorate.

Difficult Church Changes

What follows is a list of some of the most difficult changes ministers have to face in ministry. Because change dynamics contain so many variables, it's impossible to rank these changes precisely. For example, refurbishing a sanctuary may be easier to do in one congregation than another in the same community, because the first congregation uses a more comprehensive strategy of change than the second. Or again, the first congregation may have a sanctuary that had deteriorated much more than the second; thus the congregation was more motivated to renovate. Despite such variables, pastors routinely report that the following changes have been difficult:

—changing the power structure in a congregation
—merging two congregations

✗—making needed staff changes in transitional neighborhoods, like calling an African-American pastor to a previously all-white congre gation
—refurbishing a sanctuary
—moving from one location to another
—adopting a board or congregational resolution in regard to a burning social issue like war or civil rights
—voting to withdraw from the church's denomination
✓—revising the liturgy
—demolishing a revered old building used by the church since its founding
—replacing a volunteer who has served for many years, like a Sunday school teacher or church treasurer
—asking a congregation to change any time-honored church custom such as holding a bazaar as a fund raiser
—changing the method for electing congregational leaders
—establishing new patterns for grouping people in Sunday school classes
—firing an ineffective church employee
✗—ministering to new residents in a neighborhood that is changing ethnically
—replacing or not using memorial gifts donated by members, like an old KJV pulpit Bible[1]

While serving as a pastor, I had to face many of the changes outlined above. An intentional strategy for change, based on sound principles, would have helped me greatly. Fortunately, those principles and strategies are available today. Do not think, however, that change will ever become easy to effect. It's still complicated. Though knowing the complexity of change may make you less eager to engage in the process, it should help you become more effective when you do.

Strategies for Effecting Change

Change your attitude toward change! To determine your actual attitude, fill out the assessment inventory in Appendix 2. This helpful exercise will reveal your attitude. Did you discover that your attitude was fearful and pessimistic? If so, you may mightily resist change yourself. Do you not thereby betray the fact that you don't really believe change can be a sign of what God is doing in the world "to pluck up and to pull down, to destroy and to overthrow, to build and to plant" (Jer. 1:10)? As a result of probing into your own attitude, you will discover how *you* need to grow and also why *others* resist change.

The pastor who desired more frequent observances of the Lord's Supper could have petulantly threatened to resign if the board did not adopt the recommendation. She would have revealed a naive, unrealistic attitude toward change. If the issue, however, had been whether to accept an unkempt, homeless person as a member, then she might have chosen to take a brave stand for the gospel. Hence, the standard advice is: choose your battles carefully. Either a pessimistic or naive attitude can influence you to make unwise choices.

Use the opportunities you already have to create change. After all, worship services, committee structures, and board meetings are in place. So you can use them immediately without initiating a change process at all. That should partly satisfy your urge to make changes at once.

Suppose, for example, that you like neither the order of worship in your new congregation, nor its apparent indifference to the needs of the world. On the one hand, you could opt to change the order of worship the second Sunday you are there, and run the obvious risk of irritating the congregation. But you could also decide to adopt another strategy. Rather than change the order of worship, you look instead at the *present* pattern of the church's worship.

Therefore, when you include in your prayers the needs of the entire world, are you not broadening the horizons of a congregation that may have turned inward? When you indicate in your preaching that you are aware of different viewpoints on issues, are you not creating a climate for eventual change among the worshipers? Thus, without changing the order of worship, you have attempted to create an awareness of the needs of the world.[2]

Study the dynamics of change. Change technology teaches us that a *re-orienting* change, like choosing an African-American pastor for a church in a transitional neighborhood, is vastly more difficult than a *tuning* change, like servicing the copy machines regularly. It can also teach us the difference between effecting change in *anticipation* of a different future and effecting change as a *reaction* to changes in the church's

- Discuss w/PPR
- Develop a worship committee/team – discuss
- Work toward small changes over time
- W/approval, suggest a trial period
- Evaluate feedback on trial
- Modify changes

environment. As an illustration, when you study your community you see that baby boomers are moving into your neighborhood once again. You then decide to change your church programming to meet some of their needs. That's anticipatory change. But if many "For Sale" signs suddenly went up your neighborhood, you might be forced to do an in-depth study of your community. That is reactive change.[3]

So, take a class on how leaders can lead congregations in church transformation. Periodic offerings from seminaries plus organizations like the Center for Parish Development, Net Workshops, and the Alban Institute will inform you about principles and strategies you need to know. Becoming more knowledgeable about the intensity and complexity of change will enable you to apply that knowledge as you lead your new church in its ministry. *The whole point of the gospel is transformation! And this a priters emphasis*

Know your congregation. What are its customs? How have people done things before? A pledging system that worked well in your "home" church in the city, for example, may fail miserably in a small, family church.

Study the church's history. Do you recall the pastor-historian who went to work learning the history of his congregation? By enabling the members to review their past, he helped them become aware of the many changes they had *already* made in the course of their history. That realization gave them the confidence they needed to make future changes.

Also, try to discern whether any change now on the horizon for the church can be connected with an activity or program in the church's past. *Particularly in a small church, members will embrace a new proposal if they conclude that the proposal really grows out of who they are rather than constituting a new project.* *NOT REALLY "NEW"*

Lead from a pastoral base. A congregation is much more likely to accept recommendations for change from someone they have come to know, love, and trust. But how willing are some pastors to take the time needed to build such relationships? Consider the pastor who immediately became involved in the voter registration drive in his new community. Granted, his zeal was admirable, his cause good. Also, he might not ever have been able to cultivate a strong enough pastoral base for his congregation to condone his action. Still, he never gave the principle a chance to work, for he did not allow his congregation to know, love, and trust him.

If he had, they might have tolerated his social concerns, saying, "Well, you know how Martin is."

Even though you do lead from a pastoral base, it still takes time and patience to work with a congregation to see how the biblical witness stands in opposition to our culture. But is that approach not preferable in the long run?

Fill the glass slowly. Suppose you want to fill a glass with water. If you turn on the spigot full blast, you won't actually fill the glass—the water will spill over from the excessive pressure. If you fill the glass slowly, you will obtain a full glass of water. Likewise, if you desire to wear a pulpit robe in a church where it has not been customary, start by wearing your robe on a special occasion like Christmas or Easter. Your slow strategy will help the congregation accept the idea.

When I worked with the Worship Committee and my governing board in one church to develop a new liturgy, we told the congregation we would try the service for six weeks and then evaluate their responses before adopting it permanently. During that time we received excellent feedback from worshipers and incorporated many of their suggestions into the final liturgy we adopted.

Plan changes with the people. In the previous example I planned the liturgical changes with the people. The pastor who wanted more frequent communion services also continued to work with the Worship Committee on the issue. The committee then decided to ask the board's permission to observe communion on Maundy Thursday, Memorial Sunday, Homecoming Sunday, All Saints' Day, and Christmas Eve. To their surprise the board approved their recommendation. Soon people were heard saying, "We like having communion more frequently. I don't know why we haven't done it before!" As it turned out, the church was observing the sacrament almost monthly, which had been the original intent of the Worship Committee and the pastor.

Educate the congregation. Show them, as Harold Glen Brown has said, that other churches do things differently.[4] Visit other churches or circulate a questionnaire for them to fill out and return. As a case, consider an issue like changing the method of electing your church leaders, if your polity provides you with such options. When congregations discover they are only doing what many other churches have already done, some of their resistance will disappear.

Determine ways to reduce resistance to change. The prior principle of educating the congregation definitely reduces resistance. An old adage states: "People are down on what they're not up on." Talking with opponents of the change and listening to their viewpoint is basic. Finding a possible way to include them in presenting and implementing the proposal may further reduce their opposition. Closely connected with this principle is the next move.

Cultivate long-standing leaders. In small churches such cultivation is absolutely essential. No change will occur without the stamp of approval from the matriarchs and patriarchs. In churches of other sizes is it not also wise to work closely with longtime leaders? They have their time, energy, and egos wrapped up in the present status of their church. Any proposed change will threaten them. But if you talk the situation over with them and show your appreciation for their past leadership, they could come on board. And even if they don't, they might not fight the change.

Does *cultivating* church leaders seem more like *coddling* them? Perhaps, but I remember a visit I made to a church in the Florida Panhandle. The church had just decided to rotate its governing board for the first time. The clerk of the board, who had performed in that capacity for many years, said with real pain, "I can't imagine *not* being the clerk of this board!" And yet, because the pastor was very sensitive to the clerk's pain, he enabled him to stay in the mainstream of church life.

Carefully choose your first change initiatives. It is usually prudent to delay major recommendations for change for six months to a year. During that time get to know both the congregation and its mission. Obviously, the young pastor who unilaterally dismissed the pianist who was the granddaughter of the church patriarch violated this principle, as well as several others!

As you consider possible areas for change, use the suggestions in chapter 1. Also, keep the next principle before you.

Give people time and space in which to grow. One way I broach this subject with students is to ask them to identify how they have been able to change since coming to seminary. Indeed, some of them undergo dramatic changes in their attitudes, personalities, and lifestyles. Thus it is instructive for them to specify those factors that have helped them grow. "We rubbed shoulders with people of different viewpoints," says one. "We were able to discuss our views in an accepting climate," says another. "We were given space in which to grow, but it still took time," adds yet another. "Perhaps then," I reply, "it would be well to give parishioners the same opportunities to change that you have had."

Now apply this strategy to the issue of using inclusive language in the hymns. Instead of surprising the congregation in worship, the associate could have worked with people in a small group setting like a meeting of the Worship Committee. If she had begun with a clearer awareness of where people were, she could possibly have led them to a different place. While being a pastor requires such sensitivity, it does not force you to accept forever the mores of the prevailing culture as right and good. You can work for change, but do it wisely.

Test every proposed change by biblical faith. Not all change is good; therefore, we should not embrace change for the sake of change. Do we not have a responsibility to evaluate every proposal in light of our biblical tradition? Of course, you will not magically produce an isolated text to support your proposal but rather determine whether it is congruent with the sweep of biblical faith. Prooftexting—taking a verse out of context and applying it to another issue—has been widely discredited as a valid method of biblical interpretation.

Seek the presence and power of the Holy Spirit. Consider George again, the new pastor who felt his congregation had become complacent and comfortable. Perhaps for the first time he had come face to face with the famed intransigence of parish life. People do become comfortable and complacent. They resist change and want things to stay as they are.

But there is always a countervailing spirit present in parish life, the Holy Spirit. Usually there is someone, some group with whom you can work. God has not left that church without either a witness or the divine presence. Unfortunately, ministers sometimes think the church is *totally* resistant to the gospel. As we have said, they decide that their mission is to take the gospel to those "poor, misguided souls" in the parish. But the Spirit has been present, and pastors would do well to discover where the Spirit is at work.

Remember that God still rules and loves. Nothing can shake God's hold on creation. This is God's world. Though it is sometimes difficult to see how and when and where God is working, God is at work. In the words of one contemporary statement of faith:

God still works through the processes that shape and change the earth.
. . . We acknowledge God's care and control in the regularity of the universe
as well as in apparently random happenings. . . . The Creator works in all
things toward the new creation that is promised in Christ. . . . The Lord is
moving toward the time when justice will roll down like waters and
righteousness like an ever-flowing stream.[5]

And in the words of the seventh angel in Revelation, "The kingdom of
the world has become the kingdom of our Lord and of his Messiah, and
he will reign forever and ever" (Rev. 11:15). God rules!

And God loves. As Paul affirmed, nothing in all creation "will be able
to separate us from the love of God in Christ Jesus our Lord" (Rom. 8:39).
No matter what happens in our earthquake world, God's love will outlast
anything. We can remind our congregations, as well as ourselves, that God
loves us and will see us through. In the midst of change, therefore, preach,
teach, and live this message: God still rules and God still loves. The gospel
will provide a steady anchor for your people.

But as you think about change, you also become aware of the passing
of time. That brings us to a related subject: how we are managing our
time. Is time management just a question of learning a few clever
techniques or is much more involved? Chapter 7 will address that question.

CHAPTER 7

MAKING FRIENDS WITH TIME

Earlier Mary raised the question of time management in the seminar. She admitted that she had to move in part because she could no longer handle her many commitments.

When the subject of time management came before the seminar again, Jerry said, "In my first pastorate, I found I was able to spend only ten hours writing my sermons. There were simply too many demands on my time. Yet I've heard some experts say we should spend one hour of preparation for every actual minute of the sermon."

Susan asked, "You said in class one day that you once opened a horse show with prayer. I didn't say anything at the time, but that seems to me to be a terrible waste of time."

"Are there some specific tips," Frank continued, "that will help us get more done in a shorter length of time? I'm interested in working smarter, as I heard someone say, not harder."

Though most ministers have studied key biblical words for time— *chronos* and *kairos*, for example—they nonetheless raise many questions about managing their time. Like Mary they want to know how to balance numerous commitments. Like Jerry they want to know how much time to spend on sermons. Others, like Susan, want to learn how not to waste time. The rest, like Frank, want to discover how to work smarter. But questions about time management always push us to raise other questions.

As an illustration, how can anyone tell Jerry exactly how many hours to spend on a sermon? Preparing a sermon depends on many variables: your ability to exegete a text, your creative skills, the total demands your parish makes on your time, your psychological and spiritual state, your home responsibilities, the pastoral emergencies of any given week, plus the expectations of your particular parish. What is crucial is to prepare your sermons faithfully. That takes time, but the exact amount will vary widely.

Suppose Jerry begins to struggle in his second pastorate. He becomes quite confused when he tries to decide how much authority he should exercise when his board makes decisions. He doesn't know how much time to spend on visitation. He further discovers that his old pattern of procrastination has followed him yet again. In his confused state Jerry prepares sermons, though ever so slowly. His confusion spills over to color his sermons both in delivery and content. Jerry's situation causes us to look at his question from another angle. It requires more than stating how many hours are necessary to write a sermon. Rather, it challenges him to look at his life holistically.

Again, suppose Jerry's family is depressed about having to leave their previous community even though Jerry was asked to resign. Jerry may feel the pressure so acutely that he is barely hanging on. His family situation, therefore, will take extra time and drain his energy. This may be another reason he is unable to take the time he needs to prepare sermons.

Nor is it easy to answer Susan's question about opening a community horse show with prayer. On the face of it such requests from parishioners seem absurd. "Don't they know how busy I am?" we ask ourselves. When I added up the time I spent driving to the show and staying long enough to be polite, the entire process took a couple of hours. As I drove home, I was angry at myself. I should have been, for *I* was the problem. I could not say no to my parishioner, and in that case I should have.

If I had been an ardent equestrian, I might have reveled in the occasion, considered it relaxing, and been glad I accepted the invitation. I might also have accepted the invitation if it had come from a church newcomer who was establishing some initial relationships with the church and me. Each request, then, depends on a number of variables and raises other questions.

In time management seminars, it has never helped me to hear that we all have the same amount of time in a day—twenty-four hours. That's true, of course, but clergy and their ministry contexts differ so radically. One of our seminary graduates, who has an almost inexhaustible supply of energy, returned to the campus and complained that he didn't have enough to do. And he didn't, because he was working in a fifty member church that scarcely challenged him. Contrast his situation with that of another graduate who became an associate on a large church staff. As a result, he found he was working five nights a week, much to the distress of his family. Both ministers had the same amount of time, yet one was breathing hard from his ministry while the other was hardly breathing!

Whatever your context, you can become more efficient. But how?

Basics of Time Management

The first weeks of getting started in any new pastorate are filled with certain basics. You need to get settled in your home, unpack your books, organize your desk, talk over the bulletin with the church secretary (if you have one!), accept invitations to people's homes, visit shut-ins and the hospitals, plan your installation, talk with committee chairpersons, read over board minutes, plan your first three or four sermons, set up a filing system, and explore the community.

Soon, however, you settle into a routine and discover the specific tasks you have to perform *weekly* like writing a sermon, drawing up the liturgical framework for the bulletin, and visiting the sick. You also find out what you do *monthly* such as meeting with your board, writing a column for the church newsletter, serving communion to shut-ins, and attending a meeting of the local ministerial association. And you learn what you need to do *quarterly*, like attending a meeting of your judicatory.

As you engage in the above activities, you interact with people, sift through priorities, and develop work patterns that reflect your use of time. *A key question will emerge: Do you view time as friend or enemy, as gift or demand, as grace or law?*

Obviously, the best way to answer that question is to see time as friend, gift, and grace. Yet most of the time we get caught up in the "busy, busy, busy" syndrome. That syndrome, as David Steele has pointed out, is quite different from the New Testament era.[1] At that time, religious leaders tried to impress one another with stories of their righteousness, "God, I thank you that I am not like other people: thieves, rogues, adulterers, or even like this tax collector. I fast twice a week; I give a tenth of all my income" (Luke 18:11-12). But not today!

"How are things going?" we ask another minister. "Busy, busy, busy," she replies. "We're in a building campaign, four people have died in the last month, and my secretary just retired." All the while you are thinking, "That's nothing. I've given five talks in the last two weeks, conducted three weddings, and had nine people in the hospital!" When she finishes, you tick off your impressive list. So it goes whenever ministers meet. One wonders, "Are we now trying to justify ourselves with our "busy-ness" as people once did with their "righteousness"? Are we revealing that time for us is enemy, demand, and law?

Certainly no one is happy playing the busy, busy, busy game. Though we may derive momentary satisfaction from impressing others with our schedules, living the breathless life will eventually burn us out or make us very irritable. Surely Jesus intended neither result when he invited us to follow him. He found time to withdraw into the hills to pray and also to observe the lilies growing in the field. He knew how to live one day at a time. Still, my hunch is that you too will get caught up in our busy, busy, busy game and learn how to play it quite well.

The way out of this trap is not easy! If time becomes enemy, demand, and law for you, you won't be able to snap your fingers and make it friend, gift, and grace.

Does this mean striving to have little work to do, or saying, "Stop the world, I want to get off"? No, we will never be able to change the frantic pace of modern society. In ministry you can't control the number of times your telephone rings, or when people die, but you can discover how to make friends with time as you meet the pressures of the day. You can learn how to observe the lilies growing in the fields as you move around. You can find time to withdraw to your study for prayer despite the ringing of the telephone. Steadily, as you respond to grace, you will experience time as friend, gift, and grace.

Time Management Is Self-Management

The primary key to time management, then, is self-management. If you cannot manage your *self*, you will never manage time. Such is the thrust of Robert L. Randall's helpful book *The Time of Your Life: Self/Time Management for Pastors.*[2] So as your ministry develops, reflect on what is happening to you to see whether *you* are the real problem.

For example, if I always end up frantically working on my sermon into Saturday night, I am the problem. If I leave my family every evening and head for the church, I am the problem. If I can never say no to a parishioner's unreasonable request, I am the problem. If I constantly take on more work than I can manage, I am the problem. Surely, the fault lies not in the stars, but in me. I will never get a better grip on managing time until I learn this truth. Perhaps Mary, who could not juggle her many commitments, needed to examine her life in light of this principle.

Now, however, time management becomes exceedingly complicated. To deal with yourself, you need to tap the resources of the gospel. What are they? They include an understanding friend who can listen as you discuss your internal dilemmas, or an accepting therapist who can see your basic needs and hang-ups emerging as you talk through your problems, or a spiritual director who can discern God's Spirit at work in your life, or a mentor who can hear your struggles and describe ways he or she has learned to cope with the same struggles, or a small group of caring Christians who can support you in your ministry. You may resist availing yourself of any of these resources, saying, "I am too busy!"

Actually, you may not be willing to deal with yourself until your situation becomes acute. Here are some danger signals to look out for as your ministry progresses:

—thinking you are indispensable
—refusing to delegate anything to anyone
—never spending time with family or spouse
—spending time with family and spouse but regretting every minute of it
—saying "I'm always behind"
—feeling guilty when you take time for yourself
—working harder, not smarter
—having feelings of guilt when you tell a parishioner "No"

When you detect several of these danger signals, it's time to take action. Don't tell yourself you can resolve your problems by attending a time management seminar loaded with clever gimmicks to save time! To be sure, the seminar may help you identify the fact that you are the real problem. Moreover, such seminars often give you useful tips to help increase your productivity. Still, the real problem in time management lies in the realm of the *personal,* not the *technical.*

The ultimate key to self-management is to ground your life in the love of God and others. Unless you do, you will continue to live the breathless life.

To become grounded in God's love means living by grace. Jesus showed us how to do that. In fact, he is the way for us to enter God's grace. "The grace of the Lord Jesus Christ . . . be with all of you." Ministers regularly say this to congregations waiting to head for home. Isn't it strange that we do not avail ourselves of that same grace?

Jesus is our exemplar. He too was busy, besieged by the sick from various diseases gathering about him at sunset (Luke 4:40); tracked down at daybreak by the crowds who wanted to prevent him from leaving (Luke 4:42); greeted at Capernaum by a crowd that overflowed the house and by a paralytic dropped down through the roof by his friends (Mark 2:4); besought by a blind man crying out for mercy from the roadside as he was trying to leave town (Mark 10:47); hemmed in by a huge crowd but still able to perceive a touch from a woman who had been hemorrhaging for twelve years (Mark 5:30); and hounded by throngs when he and his disciples fled to a deserted place because "they had no leisure even to eat" (Mark 6:31-33).

Still, what did Jesus do in the midst of such busy-ness? He responded to each need in each moment with incredible compassion and sensitivity. The sick and lame who crowded around him at every stop, the paralytic who was dropped through the roof, or the blind beggar who cried out from the roadside, all needed help. Therefore, Jesus healed, fed, and taught as if each person was the most important person in God's kingdom. That moment, says Albert Curry Winn, "however unexpected, however demanding, was a gift from his Father to be accepted, used, enjoyed."[3]

Time for Jesus was *gift,* not *demand.* He lived life one moment at a time, one person at a time, one crisis at a time, saying, "So do not worry about tomorrow, for tomorrow will bring worries of its own. Today's trouble is enough for today" (Matt. 6:34).

Does not Jesus' example point the way for us? We cannot remove busy-ness from daily life. Yet because of our trusting relationship with God, nurtured intentionally and consistently in prayer and meditation, we can live one day at a time, one person at a time, one event at a time.

When you ground your life in God, you "strive first for the kingdom of God and his righteousness" (Matt. 6:33), as Jesus enjoined. Is it possible that our failure to use time as gift really indicates that we are not striving first for the kingdom of God? Does that in turn mean that we need to reorder our priorities and put God's kingdom first? If so, we see that the issue of time management becomes a telling clue about our spiritual state. In no way, therefore, can we resolve our spiritual state without grounding our lives firmly in God's love.

Still, there are some strategies that can help us increase our efficiency as we work. Bear in mind that it may be more difficult for persons who are *less* structured in their personalities to follow these ideas than for those who are *more* structured, love planning, and thrive on details. Even so, we can all learn how to work smarter.

Working Smarter

An important, orienting suggestion is to observe the validity of Pareto's Principle. According to his widely used theory, Vilfredo Pareto said that 20 percent of the activities you engage in—the "Vital Few" situations or problems—will produce 80 percent of your achievable results. By the same token 80 percent of the activities you engage in—the "Trivial Many" situations or problems—produce 20 percent of your achievable results. So the *significant* items in any area of activity constitute a relatively small portion of the total *items* in the group.[4] Examples of the Pareto Principle abound:

—80 percent of your reading time is spent on 20 percent of the newspaper.
—80 percent of your stewardship pledges will come from 20 percent of the members.
—80 percent of your church activities are held in 20 percent of the building.
—80 percent of your research is derived from 20 percent of your books.
—80 percent of your daily file usage comes from 20 percent of your files.

To put this in a nutshell, 80 percent of the time you expend in ministry will produce 20 percent of the results, while 20 percent of the time you expend will produce 80 percent of the results. Therefore, it's far better to concentrate on these "vital few" situations that create 80 percent of the results.

The secret, of course, lies in identifying the vital few. Anthony Arnieri has identified a number of major areas that make up the vital few for managers.[5] Though guiding a church cannot be exactly equated with serving as a manager in business, some of areas Arnieri mentioned are nonetheless similar enough to be helpful. They are:

—personal organization
—reducing task time through planned activity
—eliminating unnecessary tasks
—increasing personal output
—understanding key time management techniques

When considering *personal organization,* first decide what activities you want to accomplish each day. Then prioritize these activities in terms of the most important, second most important, and so forth. A daily plan of prioritized activities will help you stay on course for what you need to do.

Next, keep your desk, work area, and files organized for efficient daily activity.

Also, in personal organization, develop a good filing system for sermons, minutes, articles, and books. Experts estimate that we waste 20 percent to 30 percent of our time looking for things! Record the title of every sermon and talk, along with place, date, and text, in a notebook or computer file.

If you can avoid it, never fill up your daily calendar with wall-to-wall appointments. You will launch yet another version of Murphy's Law: "Everybody in your parish will want to see or call you at the same time!" As a result, you will only become tense and frustrated as the day progresses and be more likely to take it out later on your family or friends.

Determine your most productive work time. Is it morning, afternoon, or evening? It was several years before I discovered that my most productive time for sermon preparation, writing, or lecturing is in the morning. When I try to do serious work in the afternoon, I often become sleepy and unproductive. Nor can I work late at night, so I prefer to go to bed and work early the next morning. Though at times you will have to violate your body rhythm, you will do your best work when you observe it.

Your next vital few category is *to reduce task time through planned activity*. This will require you to establish short- and long-term goals, objectives, and action steps. The only way to create dynamic services of worship—your goal—is to convert your goal into concrete action steps such as working on more effective sermons and expanding the choir.

As you plan activities, remember that one hour of advance planning now may save you hours of work later. Whenever you begin planning any ministry activity well ahead of the time it is scheduled, your mind starts working on that project. Whether you are writing a sermon or a column for your newsletter or preparing for a committee meeting, you will improve your efficiency by planning ahead. By waiting until just before any scheduled event takes place to work on it, you become more prone to anxiety, which prevents you from concentrating on the task. You also discover that you can seldom find the basic materials you need to aid you in your research.

The third vital area is *to eliminate unnecessary tasks*. Your temptation will always be to get involved in unimportant activities. Fight every such temptation and concentrate on the most important aspects of ministry—where lives are hurting, where the mission of the church is at stake, where the gospel needs to be preached.

To eliminate unnecessary tasks, keep an occasional two week time log once or twice a year. By itself a time log will not revolutionize your ministry. But when you analyze the days you have broken down into fifteen-minute time blocks, you will see various patterns emerging. Notice particularly when you are doing things that others should be doing. Your refusal or inability to delegate, if it becomes habitual, may indicate a need to manage yourself better.

The fourth vital area to concentrate on is *increasing your output*. To do so requires removing any negative factors that sap your energy. Are you repressing a lot of anger toward your parishioners for not giving you a larger raise? If so, it will keep you from working productively. Learn how to deal with such frustrations either directly or indirectly—and soon. When you allow them to build up, they cripple your effectiveness.

To expand your personal output, keep abreast of all the key areas of ministry. The more knowledge you develop about pastoral care, for example, the more quickly and helpfully you can relate to any given need.

- Worship planning
- Christian education/spiritual formation
- Sermon preparation
- Pastoral care
- Organizing the parish/polity
- Theology

The fifth vital area is *understanding key time management techniques.* Among the most important is the Pareto Principle we have been considering. Remember to concentrate your efforts on the 20 percent "vital few" tasks that lead to 80 percent of the results. Thus you will learn how to run more effective meetings, make better decisions, communicate more successfully, and work with your staff more productively. Furthermore, working on a sermon during your peak times of concentration will produce far more results than working on a sermon during your down times. Making a few calls on key persons produces more results than making random calls on many. So, identify those vital few activities on which you should concentrate your energy.

Yet, be careful when you assess what activities of ministry belong to the vital few. In my five pastorates people have told me about insignificant things that I did which helped them in some way, yet at the time I would never have assigned that activity a place in the vital few. By all means change your attitude toward interruptions! While interruptions are irritating when you are concentrating on a task, they often lead to ministry. As the writer of Hebrews reminds us, "Do not neglect to show hospitality to strangers, for by doing that some have entertained angels without knowing it" (Heb. 13:2).

Thus time management comprises much more than learning a few techniques. Indeed, this area of ministry may drive you to your knees in prayer, propel you to phone a therapist, or prod you to join a Bible study group. Our next subject—stress management—may affect you similarly. In fact, managing time and managing stress are integrally related. The following chapter will help you see how.

CHAPTER 8

COPING WITH STRESS

W hat have you already learned about managing stress?" I asked the seminar group.
"I never thought I would be asked to leave my first pastorate," said Jerry. "That put me and my family under enormous stress."

The other pastors spoke of the toll that conflict, disillusionment, and family tensions had taken on them in earlier pastorates. The seniors, composed of three second-career persons, revealed their own insights.

"Let me tell you about stress," Bill, a Vietnam veteran, said. "I was a helicopter pilot and had to fly numerous missions under enemy fire."

"And as a nurse before coming here," said Susan, "I worked in a hospital emergency room in Pittsburgh for six months during my final year in nursing school. I experienced more stress in those six months than in the rest of my life put together."

I wondered initially whether I could tell them anything about stress. I was well aware that I had never been asked to resign from a church, nor had I endured the pressure of enemy fire or the tension of an emergency room. Then I remembered that I had been engaged in pastoral ministry for forty years; perhaps I could help after all.

The stressors I had seen were parishioners at each other's throats; staffs embroiled in conflict; the draining nature of inner city work; the strain of several building programs; the turmoil of social issues like Civil Rights, the Vietnam War, and school integration; intense family demands brought on by rearing three children with varying needs; moving six times; the illness and death of both of my parents and my wife; dealing with assorted parish crises ranging from attempted murder to suicide; coordinating and preaching at services averaging 600 in attendance; plus a number of personal disappointments as well.

Yet, no one lives very long without having to face stress, with some of it much more intense than mine. Looking back on my ministry after forty years, certain key lessons emerge about stress.

The Nature of Stress

Stressors in our lives vary widely. Physical danger is a stressor, as are a blow to our self-esteem, work overload, and an argument with one's spouse. Good news like receiving an exciting call puts stress on our bodies. Our bodies will react similarly to all of the above stressors, though experts say good stress—*eustress*—places far fewer demands on our bodies.

Stress reactivity is our response to stress. We tend to either fight or flee. When faced by a mugger on a dark street, fleeing, or even fighting may be appropriate. When you are bitterly criticized in public by another staff member, it is neither appropriate to flee nor to fight. Incidentally, one stress expert advises, "And if you can't fight and you can't flee, *flow*."[1] If we are unable to flow when faced with our more modern stressors, we are often left with unused products like adrenaline in our bodies.

Stress is the combination of a stressor and stress reactivity. Unless you have both, there is no stress. In other words, a stressor like a parishioner's criticism of your pastoral work has only the potential to elicit a stress reaction. Suppose two ministers lose their jobs at the same time. One is devastated and leaves the ministry, while the other learns from what has happened and continues in ministry. Jerry, who was asked to leave his first pastorate, was obviously learning much in spite of his pain.

A *strain response can determine how you are responding to stress.* Though not entirely accurate, some surveys now available can help you assess how you are holding up under the stressors in your life.[2] When administering these surveys, I have discovered each time that some people recognize that they are in trouble. At the least, some notice their strain response scores are so high that they are willing to take a deeper look at their lives. Yet other people, faced with seemingly tremendous pressure from all sides, reveal little strain in their scores. This fact suggests we would do well to examine the lives of people in both groups to discover the reasons for their divergent responses.

Pre-transitional Stress

As you begin any new pastorate, you will be under stress. The very act of negotiating with a church, accepting a call, packing up, and moving to a new place creates stress. Meeting new people each day, stewing over how to get started, wondering whether you are being well received, pondering your first sermon and initial board meeting—all create stress. If you are married, there will be additional stress because your family also has to adjust to a new situation. They may have become firmly rooted in their last community and wish they did not have to move at all. Your spouse may work and therefore must look for a new job. Your children will need to make other friends as well as attend a different school. None of this is easy. In your family discussions everyone may be saying, as did the children of Israel in the wilderness, "Let us choose a captain, and go back to Egypt" (Num. 14:4).

People in your new community, especially your church members, will be anxious to meet you and your family. That is an advantage you would not always have in another line of work. Granted if you were in another line of work you would also have to make similar adjustments. What's so difficult, then, about the stress that emerges when ministers move to a new pastorate?

Transitional Stress

Paul Dietterich has traced some characteristics of the transition state in the life of a church and a minister that illustrate the sources of potential stress.[3] His article is as apt for new ministers as it is for those moving to another pastorate. After all, newly ordained ministers will experience all of the following potential stressors for the *first* time. They will not have a backlog of pastoral experience on which to rely, saying, "This is what I did before, and it worked for me."

The first characteristic of the transition state is its uniqueness.[4] This time is different from the pre-transition state of the church, for example, because the church under the former pastor knew clearly what its structures, norms, roles, policies, and relationships were. Then, even though that state may not have been entirely satisfactory, the congregation at least had hammered out those patterns. The transition state is also different from the post-transition state that will be in place after the new pastor and the congregation forge yet another set of work patterns.

Before leaving, perhaps the previous pastor hesitated to make any long-range decisions that might tie your hands. The congregation then hesitated to make any long-range decisions until you arrived. After you arrive, *you* will rightly hesitate to make strategic decisions until you get a feel for the situation. The net result? The church may mark time with short-range thinking and planning for up to several years.[5] So the transition period is indeed unique. *post-poned decision-making*

New relationships will also characterize the transition state.[6] In this state some people will function in relationships that are different from their past relationships. Moreover, they will be different from their future relationships. As an illustration, in churches that use the process of a congregational call, the Search Committee has a much more prominent place prior to your entry than later. In churches that have a Pastor-Parish Relations Committee, such committees often play a critical role in the transition. These new and different relationships, though temporary, still create stress for the church and the new pastor as well.

Don't some members always fear that the new pastor will cause them to lose influence and power? Don't others consider leaving for fear they won't be able to function as well in the church under new leadership?

Guilt, grief, and anger further characterize the transition state. No one can ever calculate how much guilt is left over from the congregation's relationship with the former pastor. When Mary leaves a thriving parish after six years, some may feel guilty for the way they treated her. Others may wish they had done more to keep her. Still others wonder whether they tried her patience and forced her departure. In all the scenarios, *guilt* gnaws at parishioners.

Many parishioners may experience *grief* over Mary's departure. She was deeply involved in their lives, specifically in primary moments like illness, marriage, death, and divorce.

Moreover, the circumstances of a former pastor's departure may have been traumatic. In cases when pastors are fired because of moral indiscretions, the congregation often never has an opportunity to deal with either their guilt or grief. They feel guilty over forcing their pastor out, yet also feel grief because they genuinely appreciated many aspects of their pastor's ministry. *When you go into such a situation, you walk right into the middle of lives full of guilt and grief.* ACKNOWLEDGE THIS!

Some parishioners belonging to churches using a call process may even feel betrayed by a pastor's departure. When I was leaving a new church development I had served for seven years, a parishioner told me he was very angry and said I had betrayed the congregation. In fact, he left the church soon after I did. If you had followed me as a new pastor in that situation, you might have been caught in the undertow of such anger from other members who did not leave. "I don't want to establish a relationship with *any* new minister," they may say to themselves, "for they too will soon leave us."

Thus, unresolved issues from prior relationships can create enormous stress for you as you enter a new pastorate. Typical for any minister starting up is the case of a parishioner making negative remarks about the previous minister. It is wise to remember that all such triangling efforts are residue from previous relationships. The more you resist the flattery that comes from such attempts, the better start you will make in your church.

Edwin Friedman suggests that we avoid interfering with or rearranging the triangles in the established relationship system.[7] Recognize that as a new pastor you are "marrying into" a relationship system that is already established. If you enter that system and try to rearrange all the relationships, chaos will likely result. You can suggest new ideas, to be sure, but that is different from attempting to be a fixer or rearranger. If you notice a strong emotional reaction to what you perceive to be a harmless suggestion for change, the content of your suggestion is not the problem. Rather, what your suggestion portends for change in the previously existing triangles of the relationship system is the problem.[8]

Post-Transitional Stress

Role-related stress swiftly surfaces in ministry. Ministers and congregations do not always expect the same things! Michael G. McBride has said that the model pastor:

—preaches exactly twenty minutes and then sits down

—condemns sin but never hurts anyone's feelings

—works from eight in the morning until ten in the evening but never gets tired

—is 26 years old and has been preaching for 30 years

—has a burning desire to work with teenagers but spends much time with senior citizens

—makes fifteen calls a day on church members, yet evangelizes the unchurched at a record pace

—does all of the above without ever being out of the office when you call![9]

In regard to role conflict, most ministers struggle daily trying to decide which inner voice to listen to in practicing ministry. There is the *seminary voice* that stays with us, perhaps to our surprise. Even now, at this late date in my career, I still hear one of my professors saying, "Preach on a biblical text"; another saying, "Sit with your parishioners and hang out the flag that says you are willing to help"; and still another saying, "Don't worry about your yard. Let your children dig a hole to China if that's what they want to do." Those seminary voices remain powerful influences in my life, as will seminary voices in yours.

We also hear the *judicatory* voice. Sometimes this voice tells us, "Our programs are important. Please implement them in your churches." If we don't we wonder whether our judicatories will stand in the way of our "advancement" in ministry.

Moreover, don't we hear the *congregational* voice? "We want you to visit more," parishioners sometimes say. "Do you really have to spend so much time away at judicatory meetings?" they add. That too is a powerful voice, for it is spoken by people who pay our salaries and form the network in which we work every day.

Happily we also hear the *inner voice of Christ*. While listening to all the other voices, we are really seeking the voice of Christ through Scripture, prayer, and dialogue with the community of faith. "What does Christ want me to do?" we ask. "After all, I can't satisfy all of these voices. What do I need to preach about this issue, or do I preach on it at all? How do I spend my time today?" We thus search for Christ's will. For in the final analysis we have to answer to him, not seminary, congregation, or judicatory. Some of what you learn in seminary you will later decide was bad advice. Some of what the congregation tells you cannot and should not be done. Some of what you hear from your judicatory will be too demanding, even unworkable. So you feel trapped in the middle where all of the voices converge, attempting to hear the voice of Christ. It's a stressful place to be.

Further, there is *role confusion*. Similar to role conflict, role confusion for parishioners involves being perplexed over such questions as, "Who will make decisions now, and how will they be made? Will we have to clear things with the new pastor? How will this new person exercise leadership?" As the new pastor you are wondering the same things about how decisions are made, as well as about your own leadership style.

Also connected with role-related stress is *role overload*. Obviously, ministers have many different things to do—look again at the description of the model pastor. No wonder they sometimes get lost wandering around the various trails charted by their roles. Additionally, each role requires definite skill development, else a pastor will not be effective. Congregations expect competent preaching, but they also want competent pastors, competent administrators, competent teachers, and competent group leaders. Trying to juggle all of these roles and develop their skills at the same time tends to overload all faithful clergy.

Because they often feel they are living in a fish bowl, some pastors experience their self-image merging with the role they fill. "By definition," says Michael G. McBride, "a role relates to the position the person occupies and not to the person who occupies the position."[10] Many pastors find it tricky to separate their person from their position.

Clergy also have stress because people turn to them when crises shatter their lives. People cry out, asking you to help them understand why a tragedy occurred.[11] In an early pastorate I was knocked off my feet by the pain of a couple whose two-year-old son had eaten some of his father's pharmaceutical samples and died while they were still asleep. Yet that was only the beginning of the cries for meaning I would hear in the years ahead. "Why, why?" is the eternal cry of humankind. Even though we can never fully answer that question, clergy are called upon to help people endure their suffering and find the strength to live again.

Ministers have to meet many deadlines.[12] Sunday returns almost as often as the daily newspaper. Once again you are called upon to proclaim the word of God to needy hearts. That sermon deadline will even control the way you think about the calendar. You will begin to measure a month by counting the date from the first Sunday on.

All of which creates stress! Thus every minister eventually looks for resources to help manage stress in a new pastorate.

Pastoral Resources for Coping with Stress

Your goal will *not* be to eliminate stress from your life. Far from it. We need a certain amount of tension in order to perform at all. Hans Selye, a pioneer in stress management, was asked how he coped with stress. His surprising reply: "By being as busy with my work as I possibly can. I put in at least a ten-hour day—attending staff conferences, writing papers, making speeches. And far from being wearied by this schedule, I find that I flourish on it."[13]

Yet such a schedule is neither necessary nor desirable for everyone. To follow it might unduly penalize your family or burn you out. Rather, find a schedule on which you can flourish without causing you to burn out or hurting your family in the process. Here's the skeleton of a plan to follow as you work out your schedule.

Discover your own response to stress. In other words, what is your stress level? Selye counsels us to discover whether we are "racehorses" who thrive on a vigorous, fast-paced style, or "turtles" who require peace and quiet, and a more tranquil environment.[14] Obviously, ministers differ greatly. No one can tell you exactly what your level is—you know that better than anyone else. Racehorses would be frustrated by living like turtles; likewise, turtles would not long survive living like racehorses.

As your ministry unfolds in your new pastorate, listen to your body. What is it telling you? Are you sleeping well or poorly? Are you gaining or losing weight or maintaining a steady weight? Are you irritable with your family and staff? Are you repressing anger in your marriage and work? What clues is your stomach giving you? My own situation in one pastorate provides a case in point. I was working day and night organizing a new church. I loved my work, and thrived on being a racehorse. Yet increasingly my stomach was telling me I was under too much stress. Tied in knots, I went to my doctor, who offered to put me on tranquilizers. I declined, telling myself I didn't want to resort to medication. Instead, I started running once or twice a week, only a mile at first. Gradually I stepped up my mileage to three miles and ran five or six times a week. To be sure, I was still a racehorse but I had to make some adjustments to live like one! I finally discovered how to live at the stress level I preferred.

Seek balance in your life. Take time for family. If you don't, you may find your ministry crumbling around you. Even if *you* can work all the time, your *family* won't take it. Nor should they. They need *you*. Who else can read a story to your daughter at bedtime or shoot baskets with your teenage son or take your spouse out to dinner? Inwardly you may hear a voice calling you back to the church, but drown it out unless it's an emergency. You'll discover two things: first, the sheer delight of human relationships. Even now I remember the joy of crawling around on the floor chasing babies! Second, you'll never regret the time and energy you pour into family relationships. Of course, such an expenditure never guarantees healthy and successful children or spouses. But it's still the best investment you'll ever make.

Thus, in that all-important appointment book you carry around, pencil in an evening or two a week for your spouse and children. If you are single, schedule some time for your friends. The church will survive. In fact, it may even thrive.

Take time for yourself. One curse that plagues some ministers is failing to take time for themselves. Yet they too need to take a walk, look at a sunset, or fish from a riverbank. They also need to kick off their shoes and read the paper, go out to the ballpark, or read a mystery. When you do that regularly, you will return to your work with more zest than you ever thought possible.

Nobody can tell you when to take your day or days off, only that you need to take them consistently. Many ministers take Mondays off because they find that Sundays leave them exhausted. You may not find this to be the case. Other ministers defend taking off different days, from Tuesdays to Saturdays. It works for them. Yet whenever you take time off, emergencies may still arise. For doctors schedule surgeries on your day off—people die then, too. Most of the time you will be able to take your day off, and people will usually respect your schedule. Be careful to let your congregation know when you are available. Of course, don't go to the other extreme and be like a pastor who posted this notice on the study door: "Available on Tuesdays from 3 to 4 for appointments (when possible)."

Whatever you do on your day or days off should equip you to return to your work refreshed and eager to begin again. If it doesn't, discover a different way to spend your time. Some ministers enjoy playing golf immensely, while others find it creates more stress than it relieves. Determine therefore what helps you. Whether it's golf, tennis, swimming, gardening, pumping iron, walking, climbing steps, reading, or attending concerts, do it regularly.

In your search for balance, develop a "rule of life." In other words, choose some disciplines or practices that will help you grow in faith and the life of faith. A steady diet of Scripture reading, prayer, worship, witness, and service will keep your relationship with God strong. Your goal is *not* to obey your rule legalistically but to receive God's grace. When you fail to observe your chosen disciplines—as often you will—be gentle with yourself. Simply return to your rule or revise it in light of your experience.

Is not dealing with stress ultimately a spiritual problem? Like managing time, it is a matter of learning to live by grace. When grace floods our lives, we cease our anxious striving. We become steady and calm in the midst of conflict. Deadlines no longer overwhelm us. We are more likely to discern meaning in a crisis and bring hope to the forlorn. Our roles become clearer, for we are guided by Christ to discern his will for our lives.

While discussing stress management in new pastorate start-ups, we have barely touched upon several key sources of stress. Three such sources form the building blocks of the next chapter.

CHAPTER 9

FACING SPECIAL
START-UP ISSUES

In our initial discussion in the New Pastorate Start-up Seminar, Susan urged us to consider the matter of associate–senior pastor relationships. Also, as a woman in ministry, she symbolized some special issues women face in their careers.

Bill, the ex-military officer, represented a growing group of persons who have entered ordained ministry as a second or third career. Will his previous experience help or hinder him as an ordained minister, and how?

If you are neither a woman, nor an associate, nor a second career minister, *don't skip this chapter.* For one thing, men need to see how women function in ministry so they can learn from their leadership patterns. Moreover, men should study issues women face because they are directly involved in those issues. Often we men *are* the issue and until we "get it," little progress is possible. We cannot mature unless we work on the issues *together.* Then when we get it, we can begin to influence the church systems in which we work.

Also, numerous ministers will work in multiple staff relationships during their lifetime. Would it not therefore be helpful to examine some of the dynamics inherent in those relationships as one considers a new pastorate? Stan, for example, is moving to a new community where the church is bursting with growth. Before long he and the church will have to consider increasing their staff. What dynamics do they need to ponder as they prepare to expand?

A final reason for reading this chapter lies in the interconnected nature of ministry. Increasingly, you will be working with both sexes, if not in staff relationships, then certainly in your judicatories. Further, it will help you understand not only your own staff relationships but also those of the colleagues with whom you work. So what is it like for Susan to be a woman in ministry? What is it like for her to be an associate? How will Bill's military background affect him as he embarks on a second career?

Issues for a Woman Beginning a Pastorate

Women in ministry are a fact in most denominations and have been for a long time. Moreover, the percentage of women in our theological institutions continues to rise, reaching as high as 50 percent in some schools. Also, in a few places women have been called to serve as heads of staff of large churches. Even more have been called as solo pastors. Many serve as associates. Still others are serving in judicatory positions. So, with such a rosy outlook, why bother with the subject at all?

Despite the clear progress the church has made, too many women in parish ministry have reported serious difficulties for us to dismiss the subject as a waste of time. *Not* to discuss these issues would constitute a critical omission.

We can accurately say that the experience of women in ministry is similar to, yet different from, the experience of men. If women get in touch with the similarities in all ministries, then they won't feel quite so isolated and alone. If women can also see where their issues are different, then both sexes need to become aware of them. Because of space constraints, we look at only one major issue here: leadership—comprising style, power, and authority.

An emerging consensus agrees that women work from a different paradigm when they provide leadership. Concisely put, the paradigm states that women are relational and collaborative when they work with others. They are interactive, share power and information, enhance other people's self-worth, and get others excited about their work.[1] As Sally Helgesen says, *women are weavers,* who make connections and weave a "web of inclusion" in the workplace.[2] Women tend to move toward consensus by working from experience. Whenever they work from experience, they are concerned about relationships, process, and interaction.

Of course, this leadership style preferred by females is not practiced exclusively by women. Not all women work from this paradigm, while some men do. In fact, Rensis Likert and his associates at the University of Michigan identified many of these same characteristics in researching the most effective managers in North American business and industry. Likert called such managers *supportive* leaders, for they worked collaboratively with others, were open and receptive to new ideas, and helped people with their work. Again, management theorist W. Edwards Deming taught a similar style by calling for more team building and relational management in the workplace.[4]

For many years I have taught that supportive leadership that is relational and collaborative is the most effective leadership style for church leaders. Moreover, the supportive leader stunningly resembles the servant leader that Jesus both modeled and taught his disciples to emulate when he said, "The greatest among you must become like the youngest, and *the leader like one who serves*" (Luke 22:26, italics mine).

But a supportive, servant leadership style may be problematic for both men and women. Have not men led more often by exercising "power *over* others" than "power *with* others"? Feminists also, says Lynn N. Rhodes, "are deeply suspicious of images of service and servanthood."[5] She believes "the concept of a ministry of service continues to be used to disempower laity, especially women, and to justify clergy use of power by calling it servant leadership."[6] Further, she has pointed out how ideas of service have been interpreted differently for men and women in the church. Also, as Celia Hahn states:

> Under the soft blanket of "service," feelings of worthlessness often hide. Hungry for the caring and affirmation she isn't getting, the maternalistic woman fills her own void by taking care of others—whether they want it or not. Her "service" parodies the serving that freely responds to the perceived needs of others. Thus she has other tasks to perform before "servanthood" becomes an appropriate ideal.[7]

As a result of male domination, Rhodes says that women "do not know how to talk about love, service, vulnerability, caring."[8] Some women leaders even fear becoming vulnerable because male leaders have previously seen the vulnerability of women as weakness and have discredited them. Rhodes urges the church to reject dominating power and to affirm shared power, which is essential in order to analyze any established authority. It's not that power itself is evil; rather, power over others is evil.[9] She argues that the challenge for feminists is to address the church's involvement in power over others and, at the same time, not be trapped in subservient roles. She wants the church to see service as the empowerment of others.[10]

Herein precisely lies the problem for women in ministry. The prevailing white male system of "power over others" is still the norm in the church as well as everywhere else. Hence, what does a woman minister do? Does she buy into the white male system to gain acceptance? Or does she lead from the feminine, "power with others" paradigm she is more likely to embrace?

The dilemma is real. If a woman tends to exercise power as many men do, she will be criticized as too aggressive. A man, however, who exhibits similar behavior is often praised as a strong leader.

On the contrary, if a woman leads from a feminine paradigm, she will be judged to be weak and ineffective by males who operate from a different paradigm. Whatever a woman does, it seems she cannot win!

Carol E. Becker says that the "most critical barrier for women is the inability of the white male to recognize and value the feminine paradigm for leadership."[11] Many men are either uncomfortable or unfamiliar with the feminine style. Of course, some men, as we have seen, do value the feminine paradigm, but "men and women working together in the church get caught trying to be collaborative in systems that remain hierarchical."[12]

Thus the church must continue to dismantle its hierarchical leadership. *While it does, the church should use the language of servanthood and authority very carefully so as not to perpetuate male domination over women.* Also, the church needs to understand that only when a sense of abundance replaces a woman's inner impoverishment, as Celia Hahn says, will "service that is perfect freedom become a possible and appropriate task for her."[13] The church would also do well to emphasize service as the empowerment of others, working to change power relationships.

Even so, the church cannot abandon servanthood as the foundation of its authority or as the purpose and pattern of its ministry. Was not servanthood the basis of everything Jesus said and did? "I am among you as one who serves" (Luke 22:27), he *said.* Stooping to wash his disciples' feet is what he *did*. He called upon the disciples "to wash one another's feet" (John 13:14). Is not Jesus' word a mandate for all?

As a result, servanthood will continue to require Christian leaders to demonstrate vulnerability, self-sacrifice, and caring. Quite simply, servanthood is the essence of the church and its ministry. Yet it strongly calls upon *all* church leaders to be servants, particularly males. For male leaders to use servanthood language as a mask for maintaining power over women is unconscionable.

Thus a key leadership issue for women as they move to a new pastorate continues to be the issue of power. Women may not "recognize that power over others is a fundamental value in the white male system and that all work is a struggle for some kind of power. For men operating within the system, however, power is the source of their authority."[14] If a woman threatens the power of men by raising issues, "The response of the men is swift and brutal: Cut off her power!"[15]

To set off such a violent explosion, a woman associate does not have to threaten the power of the male head of staff, only the power of men in key leadership positions. One such woman said she was asked to leave when she raised a question about the propriety of a church fund-raiser that was led by a male. In her case the senior pastor was "powerless" to stop her dismissal.

In other cases when women associates have been asked to leave a church, they may not have raised any issues with the church itself. Rather, the head of staff himself was the problem. One woman associate, who was treated badly by a tyrannical senior pastor, discussed her situation with the church staff committee, then with the proper judicatory committee. The outcome was predictable: the prevailing white male power structure in both the board and judicatory reluctantly sided with the head of staff, and she was asked to start looking for another call. Again, power over others is the source of white male authority.

Even when women serve as heads of staff in churches and judicatories, they encounter the same problem of power in working with their boards and councils. For they work from one conception of power while those they work with may operate from a white, male perspective.

Should women then acquiesce and replicate the leadership style of men? No, women have many gifts to offer the church through their own preferred leadership style. Are risks involved in adhering to their more relational, collaborative, empowering style? Yes, but the risk to the church is even greater if they do not use their style, because their style is exactly what the church desperately needs to see modeled today!

Moreover, should women adopt a personal, feminist agenda in a new pastorate that they should pursue at all costs? Of course, every woman— and every minister for that matter—must retain certain core beliefs that define who they are as Christians. Yet they must be careful not to make *everything* a core issue. One woman, who has wrestled deeply with this problem, said, "My agenda is the gospel. I don't have a personal agenda. Instead, I ask myself, 'How do I show God's love in this situation?' My call from God is so clear. I'll be true to that call." She added that when she was true to her call, she believed God would use her and see her through. By no means has her perspective protected her from being hurt by predominantly white male leadership behavior. But it has enabled her to persevere and to provide a strong witness for others.

Beginning a Pastorate as an Associate

In a sense we have anticipated some of the issues involved when one becomes an associate. Already it has become clear that power is a key issue in many staff relationships, those including male as well as female associates. Yet power alone does not describe all of the difficulties inherent in multiple staff ministry.

I began my ministry as an assistant pastor. That brief experience left me with vivid memories of how difficult staff relationships can be. When I later became a head of staff myself, I soon developed much more sympathy for anyone in that position. The fact remains that all positions in multiple staff ministry are laden with potential problems.

The specific issues in multiple staff ministry are common and well-known. Associate pastors frequently share the following remarks with one another:

"The head of staff is power mad. He has to control everything."
"He uses all the right words about team ministry, but doesn't know the first thing about being a team member."
"He won't spend the necessary time for us to develop good staff relationships."

"He won't let me do anything like baptisms and preaching, except when he needs a break or is out of town. Therefore, I feel like a second-class citizen."

"I get blamed for everything that goes wrong around here, and *he* dropped the ball, not *me!*"

"He's a workaholic and expects us to be workaholics too. Well, I refuse, and I know it causes him grief." (Most heads of staff are male; hence the masculine language.)

But heads of staff have their concerns too:

"The associate seems to think all I have to do is sit around at staff meetings and talk. She doesn't realize the demands on my time."

"He doesn't have a clue what it would be like to have all the responsibility in this church. He only has to work with the youth, and that's it."

"I don't know what she does with her time. Seems like she's hardly ever here, yet she talks about how overworked she is. I don't understand it."

"He doesn't take the time to ask questions about things he knows nothing about. Rather, he gets on his horse and rides off in all directions. And I have to pick up the pieces."

"This relationship is just not working out. I don't know whether we should terminate him now or later."

"Frankly, she's incompetent and doesn't seem to know what she's doing. And she went to the same seminary I did!"

On and on heads of staff go as they give their slant on staff difficulties.

Is there anything you can do to sidestep some of the pitfalls and ensure that your staff relationships will at least have a chance to be fulfilling? The suggestions that follow will assist you when you think about becoming part of a multiple staff ministry.

The key to having good staff relationships lies primarily with heads of staff. If they are mature, have a secure sense of self, and are growing in grace, then they will establish a climate in which good team relationships can develop. I say "can" develop because the process is by no means automatic. Other dynamics come into play as well, many of which are not and cannot be determined by the senior staff member.

Every member of the staff has important responsibilities to carry out in an effective team ministry.

But how can a prospective associate find out about the maturity of the senior staff member when considering a move? If there have been any previous associates, talk to them to find out their previous experiences with staff relationships. Also, talk to other pastors in the community and judicatory officials as well. Does the church have a revolving door for associates? Gradually you will pick up significant threads about the senior staff member's ability to work with people. In chapter 3 we saw Kevin doing his homework on Jacob, the head of staff for Trinity Church, and it paid off for him.

Study family systems theory. In dealing with previous issues like conflict in chapter 5, we noted how systems theory applies to churches. The theory is especially useful in looking at staff relationships. As an example, a senior staff member and board may have trouble relating. So to stabilize their relationship they begin to focus on the associate. As a result, the associate can do nothing right in the senior staff member's eyes. Nor can the board see much good in the associate's work either. They continue to find fault with the associate instead of honestly facing the problems they have in working together. Studying other nuances of systems theory will be fruitful for any staff person.

Learn as much as you can about collaborative ministry. Granted, you may have to start learning such principles *after* difficulties begin to surface in your parish. But where goodwill exists among staff members, a retreat or conference or regularly scheduled visits by a consultant can mitigate the difficulties. One associate says that the best thing her staff ever did was to receive some coaching from an outside consultant. He enabled them to come to grips with themselves individually and corporately as they groped for some solid footing in the quicksand of their dynamics.

Another associate says a staff retreat paved the way for more constructive relationships to develop. All members had an opportunity, in a non-threatening atmosphere, to put their concerns on the table. In her case the senior member was a good leader and truly wanted the staff to work together as a team. Otherwise, the retreat would never have worked as well.

I have developed a tool that enables staff members to reveal their perceptions of how effectively they are working together. (See Appendix 3.)

In one consultation I asked the senior staff member how well he thought his staff was working together. He gave each category very high marks—at the *top* of the scale. When I asked the associates how they ranked their effectiveness and relationships, they disclosed scores at the *bottom* of the scale. The astonished senior staff member had not been aware of what was going on right before his eyes. Yet once their divergent levels of satisfaction surfaced, the staff began to work together more realistically.

Develop a covenant partner in ministry.[16] For further support and reflection on your unfolding ministry, meet with a senior pastor in another context or with an associate pastor. I prefer meeting with an understanding senior pastor simply because his or her perspective on ministry will be different from yours. You will therefore see the actions and needs of your own head of staff more sympathetically. On the other hand, when two associates meet as covenant partners, they are more likely to meet and gripe about how awful their staff relationships are, rather than moving toward better work arrangements.

Another tool to use when problems occur is a key list used to prioritize ministry concerns. Each member of the staff should complete the form and then share it with the head of staff. (See Appendix 4.)

Of course, the senior staff member would need to be willing to discuss this survey with you and to take it seriously. Only then could you mutually agree on some changes in your job description to propose to your church staff committee and official board. Ideally, it would be better for the senior staff member to invite *you* to fill out the survey. But in such situations the initiative for change often has to come from associates.

Although from an associate's perspective you might want almost a co-pastor relationship with the head of staff, it probably won't happen. Once again, multiple staff relationships are filled with all kinds of dynamics, including many power issues. You can reduce the difficulties, but never eliminate them.

From One Ministry to Another: Second Career Issues

A phenomenon across North America has been the increasing number of second career persons showing up on seminary campuses. In our institution the number has hovered around 50 percent, thus causing a rise in the average age of our students. As the trend continues, the church is finding that second career people bring not only rich gifts but often a valuable background from their other career.

Sometimes the background of the second career person is directly applicable to ministry, as in the case of a former personnel director. "I value my first career immeasurably," he said. "The problem solving skills I learned in business have helped me greatly." A teacher may come to seminary already possessing considerable skills in communication and writing. To be sure, she faces much work ahead to learn how to work with biblical texts, but her background will prove nonetheless helpful.

At other times a person's background may be indirectly applicable as when an accountant comes to seminary already equipped with the requisite knowledge to read church financial statements.

Moreover, the previous experience of second career persons *in the church* prior to coming to seminary can be enormously helpful. They understand church programs and processes in depth; they also understand life from the perspective of the pew. Their experience in the church and in another career provides a different context for theological education to occur. Above all, they want the seminary community to value their experience and maturity.

For some second career persons the biggest struggle comes when they move to the seminary, not when they enter parish ministry. A former banker described a cool fall day when he was walking home from class. "I remember saying to myself, 'If these folks had to make it in the real world, they would be lost. I know this is where you want me to be, Lord, but I can't deal with this. I need help.' " Help was soon forthcoming, for he was offered a job in a local church where he could earn some money and enter "the real world" again.

His struggle touched upon yet another difficulty for second career persons. Many have not only had careers, but families and homes as well. Moving to a seminary therefore entails a much more drastic adjustment for them than for a single student just out of college. They may have to sell their homes—not always an easy task—and help the total family adjust to their new situation. Another frequent adjustment is a spouse who finds a job outside the home even though he or she did not work before.

Still other second career persons experience their greatest struggle *after* they enter the pastorate. Suddenly life as a minister is not exactly the way they pictured it when they were laypersons in the church. So much more conflict occurs behind the scenes than they ever anticipated. They miss having an occasional free weekend; they feel as if they are living in a glass house; and they find it much harder to live on a pastor's salary than the $65,000 to which they were accustomed. More than one person who changed careers has second-guessed a decision to become an ordained minister. Not surprisingly, some soon return to their former careers.

But not all. Many thrive in ministry and report having their calls confirmed and their lives fulfilled at last. Though they may serve in ministry only twenty or thirty years, rather than forty, they nonetheless contribute significantly to the church.

Most second career ministers can readily relate to the life of their parishioners. Said one, "If a parishioner sleeps late one Sunday morning and begins apologizing to me, I say, 'I know you have only one day to sleep late.'" He also added, "Being a second career person affects the way I preach, too. I preach shorter sermons!" An ex-realtor added, "I understand the life situation of my parishioners."

Thus the changing nature of ordained ministry has created some special issues. In the meantime all ministers need to learn how to develop. What is required to be become a faithful and effective practitioner of ministry? We probe for answers in our final chapter.

CHAPTER 10

DEVELOPING AS A MINISTER

As a final class exercise I invited the New Pastorate Start-up Seminar to picture themselves in ministry ten years from now. "What will you be doing?" I asked.

"I guess," said Stan, "that after I serve one more congregation I would like to be pastor of a really large church, say of 1,000 members."

"Not me," said Bill. "Through my supervised ministry in Middletown last summer, I came to love the small church. I expect to be serving a small church somewhere."

"It's hard to say," said Susan. "I understand that the second move is usually more difficult for a woman. But I would like to be a solo pastor someday. I don't think I will remain an associate for the rest of my life."

Gradually each person revealed a dream, and their dreams varied widely. Based on past experience I knew that some would leave ordained ministry altogether, others would find their dream impossible and become discouraged, and still others would achieve their earlier dream. No one, of course, can accurately predict whose dreams will ever become reality.

Whether your dreams ever come true in ministry, you need to keep four aspects of ministry in tight focus: a guiding image, an evolving plan, a strengthening fellowship, and a nourishing Center. Focusing on these four aspects of ministry will help you stay the course. More than that, you will become increasingly faithful and effective as you serve.

A Guiding Image

Why are images so influential for us in ministry? First, as Donald Messer says, "Images can inflame the imagination and provide identities beyond simply filling offices or fulfilling role expectations."[1]

Early on the servant leader image inflamed my imagination and helped me see who I was. We were organizing a new church on a beautiful piece of property in Virginia. The beauty of the property was marred by one disturbing fact: it was located next door to the home of a man who was alleged to be the county's most notorious bootlegger. When we were naming the church, some quipped that we ought to call it, "The Little Church by the Still!" Beneath my own embarrassment I could hear Jesus saying, "I am among you as one who serves" (Luke 22:27).

Thus, prodded by Jesus' words, I paid a call on the alleged bootlegger and invited him and his family to come to church. I wish I could tell you that they showed up at church the following Sunday, were converted, gave up bootlegging, and lived happily ever after. To my knowledge that never happened. Even so, my guiding image of ministry was powerful enough to inflame my imagination and to remind me that as pastor, I was servant first.

Images do even more. Messer further says that they "enable us to find a sense of direction or organizing motif for our communities of faith in the world."[2] Many churches flounder, hardly knowing why they exist except to baptize, confirm, marry, and bury people. While those activities are necessary, churches still need a more dynamic organizing motif. I found that motif for the church's mission in Jesus' servant example and challenge.

Of course, the image you choose to steer your ministry may be quite different from mine. Are you in the words of Henri Nouwen a "wounded healer," able to use your personal struggles as sources of healing for others? Or, are you a "political mystic," able to combine personal disciplines of grace with a desire to change the world? Or, are you an "enslaved liberator," who though a prisoner of our affluent culture still seeks to point out an alternative way of living to our culture? Or again, are you a "practical theologian," who engages in critical reflection on the action of the church in the world?[3] Which contemporary image has God placed before you as you have studied Scripture, reflected on your life, thought about your heroes and heroines of the faith, and lived your life?

The image you choose can be invaluable as you lead a church. For example, one clergy couple has organized a new church around the motif of providing a "prophetic presence" in their community. The motif is even furnishing the impetus for a Doctor of Ministry dissertation. So, discover what your image is, develop it, build upon it, and share it. It will empower you for ministry.

An Evolving Plan

Many people leave seminary quite tired of reflecting critically, writing papers, jumping through ordination hoops, and reading a hundred pages of theology every night. In fact, they say, "My theological education ought to be able to last a long time. I'll just coast along for awhile."

Without new learning, however, any professional person soon becomes incompetent. Would you entrust a nagging stomach problem to a doctor who had skipped all medical symposia for the last five years and had read no recent research articles on gastro-intestinal disorders? No, yet many ministers studiously avoid continuing education events sponsored by their theological schools and denominations.

A disciple, *mathètes* in Greek, is a *learner* or *pupil*. All disciples keep on learning from Jesus to whom they have pledged their love and loyalty. To the Twelve, Jesus said, "When the Spirit of truth comes, he will guide you into all the truth" (John 16:13). Thus a disciple is not a onetime learner but a lifetime pupil.

Our Christian knowledge, therefore, is not something we can bottle and say, "Here it is; this is all I will ever need to know." Rather, it is living knowledge we continue to rethink and enlarge as we yoke ourselves to Jesus and live out our lives as his disciples. In the process we reflect on our lived experience. We talk with others about how they have experienced the gospel. We seek wisdom from a variety of sources to learn what new truth Jesus would teach us through his Spirit.

Yet, even when committed to continuing education, it is still difficult to devise a plan and follow it. In the midst of many pastoral concerns, you will be tempted to say, "I simply can't take the time." Often ministers proffer such excuses to escape the rigors of further education.

Suppose you are convinced you need to devise a plan for lifelong learning. What is next? Decide that you will study *daily.* As you read the morning newspaper, note events and stories that can illustrate your preaching. For example, in today's newspaper I noticed that New York Mills, a community of 972 persons in west central Minnesota, will be hosting a metaphysical discourse. The question? Does life have meaning, and if so, what is it? Such an illustration provides the very introduction I need to preach on the question, "What must I do to inherit eternal life?" Clip such stories and file them for future reference.

Moreover, continue to read a current book on a topic of ministry. What you studied in seminary may remain foundational for you; yet it needs to be updated and compared with what the Spirit is saying to the church today. One day you may read only a few pages, another a whole chapter, but you will enrich your understanding of ministry as you study.

Further, decide that you will study *weekly.* A lectionary study group of peers is the most popular weekly study currently available. Though not directly related to the personal needs of ministers, a lectionary group indirectly strengthens many participants as they share experiences and insights.

Decide also that you will study *monthly.* Establish a study group of peers to meet once a month, inviting a different person to present a case for group reflection. In a time of much church and social conflict, such a group can provide a source of constant professional growth and support. The format is as follows: the presenter either writes up a report or presents it orally to the group. Then the group responds to this question: What stirred within you as you heard the report? As the group comments, the presenter listens but does not respond. Next, after sufficient discussion has taken place, the presenter responds to the comments, clarifying what has happened, answering further questions, and asking for additional input. This relatively simple method of group study can furnish amazing insights to both the presenter and the participants.[4]

An alternative model for monthly group study is for the presenter to prepare a one page, single-spaced case study of a parish situation. The presenter divides the report into four sections: (1) the *background* of the event; (2) a *description* of what happened; (3) a preliminary *analysis* by the presenter; and (4) a personal *evaluation* of what might have been done in the situation. The group, after studying the presenter's report, gives its own analysis and evaluation. Again, the process often evokes stunning insights.[5]

A variation of the above model features a group that includes a trained psychologist or pastoral counselor. A group limited to six, for example, meets weekly or bi-monthly. Participants present situations emanating from any of the following "families": (1) individuals, couples, or families from the congregation or community; (2) the minister's work family: staff, official boards, associations, and committees; and (3) the minister's own family and personal relationships. All ministers are involved in these three family systems at all times and unresolved issues in any one of these families can adversely affect the other two. The group responds helpfully to personal situations while the psychologist or counselor facilitates the process, offering insights along the way. Such groups offer a more structured way of dealing with personal and corporate isolation, though they usually involve paying the expenses of the counselor.[6]

In addition to monthly and weekly study, decide to study *annually.* Denominations, theological schools, retreat centers, and ecumenical institutes afford exciting contexts for further work and offer everything from continuing education courses to advanced degrees. To choose what you will study, analyze your emerging gifts and weaknesses. It's best to concentrate most of your energy on developing and employing your spiritual gifts. Your gifts represent how God has particularly equipped you for ministry. *In those God-given gifts lie your greatest potential contribution to the church and the world.* So identify your gifts, whether preaching, pastoral work, administration, or service.

By no means, however, should you ignore opportunities to deal with your weaknesses as they surface. While you won't expend your major energy on them, be alert to the rough edges that block you from ministering effectively. If you hear loud and clear feedback that your preaching needs more work, attend a preaching workshop. If you hear remarks like, "Sally is a good pastor, but a poor administrator," take a refresher course in administration. Certainly listen to your own intuition that tells you when and where you need help.

Thus annually you have a marvelous opportunity to use your continuing education time. As you do so, be careful to work out the details with your personnel committee and your official board. Though they may not have to approve the leave if it is granted in your call, you should at least include them in your preliminary planning and subsequent reporting.

A Strengthening Fellowship

All who have ever engaged in ministry have had days of genuine discouragement, profound doubt, and searing pain. When you do, may you not succumb to what Richard C. Meyer describes as the "Gospel of Rugged Individualism": "Don't let anyone get too close. Make it on your own. Sharing your hurts, doubts, and weaknesses is reserved for your family only."[7] On the contrary, find help. If not within your denomination, find help ecumenically. Ministry is too complex and demanding for any of us to think we can make it by ourselves. Did not God place us in the body of Christ, a community of sisters and brothers? Without that body to help us, our growth will grind to a halt.

Concisely put, support groups function as security blankets, anchors, and cattle prods.[8] Sometimes you merely need persons to be *security blankets* who give you strength when you have been battered and bruised. At other times, you want the group to be an *anchor* to hold you steady when you are rocked by waves of change and turmoil. At still other times you desire for the group to function as *cattle prods* to confront you and get you moving when you are lethargic.

Support groups vary widely. Some books suggest many different support groups—one for personal isolation, one for understanding the community, one for establishing better relationships with the church, and one for the need for a mentor and a spiritual director. If you took part in all of them at the same time you would have little time for ministry! So, as your ministry continues to develop, recognize your most pressing needs for support and address them first.

As you cast about for support, *don't forget your own congregation.* Some, however, oppose having friends within the church. "You can't bring the judgment of God on them," a professor once said to a seminary class. The Word of God stands over against both our parishioner friends and us at times. So we always need to apply Scripture to all of us. To oppose having friends in the church is unrealistic and deprives ministers of what is natural and good. Informally, I was always strengthened by members of every church I served. A prayer breakfast on Saturday mornings with a group of men provided immeasurable help at one time. I further received strength from the small sharing groups I belonged to within several churches.

As far as your relationship with your own congregation is concerned, consider the Pastor-Parish Relations model used widely by the United Methodist Church and other bodies today. It normally consists of seven church members, one of whom can speak for the spouse (if needed), one who can speak for the pastor, one from the board who can deal with manse or parsonage issues, one from the official church board, one from the finance committee who can deal with the pastor's compensation, one from the original call committee, and one person-centered member who can effectively chair the committee. Monthly topics vary from discussing the concerns of the pastor's family, to compensation issues, to housing issues, to mutual expectations of pastor and congregation.[9]

Another type of pastor-congregational group, as suggested by Roy Oswald, consists of three or four church members who know the parish well. You choose them, but not from the official board, which only serves to approve a list of potential names. Again, the group can meet weekly or bi-monthly, possibly late in the afternoon for 45 minutes or so before dinner.[10]

Still, to deal with personal pain and isolation, *it's far better to have a group of people outside the church.* Don't air all of your dirty laundry before the congregation, but be sure to find a washing machine somewhere. You may choose, for example, to meet with a group of colleagues who offer helpful support. In Norfolk, Virginia—my third pastorate—I met with ten or twelve pastors for lunch every Thursday, rotating churches monthly. After eating as a group, we split up in dyads or triads to talk specifically about our prayer concerns and to pray for one another. Those friends sustained and supported me during some days of genuine discouragement. In the best sense, they formed a support group for me long before we had ever heard the term.

Other models abound for personal pain and isolation. A recent seminary graduate wrote me that he has started a support group for local ministers in his area. Six ministers are involved, and they meet twice a month for an hour and a half to discuss a book they have been reading plus whatever has been going on in their lives. During the past year, one member was suddenly fired after serving a congregation quietly for over fifteen years. The ministers therefore spent much time discussing the fired minister's feelings of anger and alienation. My correspondent added, "His experience sent a chill through all of us, and we want to learn from him."

Two other forms of personal and professional support deserve strong mention: *mentoring and spiritual guidance*. As for mentors, many judicatories now assign a more experienced minister to be a friend and confidant to new ministers. A mentor can tell you what is wise in ministry, and especially where the booby traps are located. (One of the dumbest things I ever tried to do was to completely unify the church budget in my second pastorate.) I recommended that the women's organization eliminate their individual budget that they raised from circle offerings. No matter how lofty my principles or how logical my thought, I revealed an ignorance about church systems. Talking that over beforehand with a mentor would have helped me see that I would create a firestorm!

Previously most of us *informally* sought more experienced pastors to talk with about our dilemmas, conflicts, and future directions. After the firestorm over the women's budget, one minister in particular filled that role for me. He probably never thought of himself as a mentor, nor I as a "mentee." Yet that was the nature of the relationship, because I knew I needed his wisdom. Today's more formal mentoring processes at least ensure the probability that seasoned pastors, as well as new pastors, will have wise counsel when they need it.

The growing presence of spiritual guides among Protestants solves two basic needs in ministry. The first and foremost need it meets is to provide ongoing guidance in spiritual growth. The second need it addresses is to offer strength in times of emotional stress. While spiritual guidance and therapy are not the same, guidance can provide the support pastors need in order to face their problems. Moreover, it offers them strength as they face their problems.

A Nourishing Center

To move toward your dream, you will also need a nourishing Center. That Center obviously is the God you have come to know through Jesus Christ.

John pushed his chair back, took another swig of coffee, and sighed wearily. He knew he was in trouble, and almost burned out by an exhausting schedule. "When did I last pray?" John asked himself. "When did I last reflect on my relationship with God?" John realized that the faith he preached—"life empowering" faith he called it—was slowly ebbing out of his own life. "What a terrible thought," John mused. "I am *denying* the faith with my life even as I *preach* the faith with my lips."

An isolated case? No, for many ministers will tell you their core faith lacks vitality. They say they have burned up all of their spiritual reserves. They are running on the fumes, waiting only to hear the last chug of their spiritual engines. That is especially tragic for anyone committed to the task of leading others to grow in the Christian life. Does not a vital ministry require a nourishing Center?[11]

But isn't it presumptuous to remind ministers that they need to stay close to Christ? Perhaps, but I am increasingly persuaded that the lack of a nourishing Center is the root cause of much ministerial discouragement and burnout. Without a growing relationship with Christ, we begin to live a "do-it-yourself" life, cut off from the Christ we intend to serve. Oh, for a while we may return to the ancient disciplines of the church that have nurtured many in the faith—prayer, Bible study, and meditation—but then for reasons we never fully understand we begin to drift away from that nourishing Center. Yet we don't intend to at all.

Thus we find ourselves grinding it out as if there were no nourishing Center, as if we were all alone in a cold, uncaring universe. We begin to seal off our inner life from others, hoping they will not see our spiritual poverty. We feel breathless and empty. And no wonder. We have cut ourselves off from Christ. Apart from Christ we can do nothing. It's so simple that we think we'll never forget it again, but we do—time and time again.

In those moments when we realize what has happened to us, we return to Christ, the nourishing Center. We confess that we have drifted away and receive his forgiveness. We ask him to help us become vulnerable, knowing how vulnerable he was even though it meant being misunderstood and rejected. We ask him to give us patience as we work with people who are not always smiling and lovely. We ask him to help us accept others as he has accepted us. We ask him to help us love others as he has loved us. Most of all, we express a strong desire to stay close to that nourishing Center—to Christ.

Therefore the task before you as you move to a new pastorate is to sustain a vital, growing faith. Many opportunities and methods exist to help you. Basically they boil down to what you yourself can do to respond to God's grace and what you can do with others. You need both.

On your own, be ever attentive to the nourishing Center in your life. Begin each day by dedicating your life and ministry to God anew. As you wake up in the morning, repeat to yourself, "This is the day that the LORD has made; let us rejoice and be glad in it" (Ps. 118:24). Far from being shallow self-hypnosis, this simple affirmation will firmly anchor you for the day.

Do not stop there. Learn to pray the Psalms. Read one each day and meditate on its truth. Write down or commit to memory a key verse like, "O my strength, I will sing praises to you, for you, O God, are my fortress, the God who shows me steadfast love" (Ps. 59:17). Let that verse reverberate in your consciousness all during the day while you visit a hospital patient or counsel a grieving widower. To be sure, for minutes, even hours, the verse may wane in your memory, but persevere. Gently bring it back to awareness and allow it to continue to empower and guide you.

Of course, you will want to supplement your reading of the Psalms by drawing on other passages from both testaments. First allow Scripture to penetrate your life and speak to you in the innermost recesses of your being. Then you can worry about whether it will preach.

Occasionally practice a contemplative reading of Scripture. As you read the story of the sinful woman at Simon's house in Luke 7:36-50, for example, identify with one of the characters in the story. It may be the woman, "who was a sinner" (Luke 7:37), Simon the Pharisee, Simon's dinner guests, or Jesus himself. Then look at the story through that person's eyes. Write down what you are feeling through that identification. Ask yourself why you chose that person. Further, ask how God is speaking to you in this story. Finally, what question would you ask Jesus if you were the only person left at Simon's house that day?

Surely, you will close your devotional time with prayer. Particularly on days when you are tired and discouraged, enumerate your blessings before God in a season of thanksgiving. There's no better way to change your mood from self-pity to gratitude.

Your dream may die or begin to fade. Conflict may boil around you. You may feel like an utter failure and question your call. What then when the lean days come?

Continue to stay close to Christ, the nourishing Center. When you do, you will know who you are and whose you are. You will be anchored to the one who said, "Remember, I am with you always, to the end of the age" (Matt. 28:20). His presence will be enough.

APPENDIX 1

HOW ARE WE
WORKING TOGETHER?

Analyze your group by rating it on a scale from 1 to 7, with 7 being what you consider to be ideal. Circle your preference. Then discuss together each item. Take special note of those items for which the average rating is below 5, or for which the range of individual ratings is very wide. Formulate some ideas as to *why* these perceptions exist.

1. Feel satisfied with the group's progress so far.
Dissatisfied   Satisfied
/ 1 / 2 / 3 / 4 / 5 / 6 / 7 /

2. Feel free to express my ideas.
Dissatisfied   Satisfied
/ 1 / 2 / 3 / 4 / 5 / 6 / 7 /

3. Feel my ideas and opinions are heard.
Dissatisfied   Satisfied
/ 1 / 2 / 3 / 4 / 5 / 6 / 7 /

4. Feel satisfied with the way decisions are made.
Dissatisfied   Satisfied
/ 1 / 2 / 3 / 4 / 5 / 6 / 7 /

5. Feel there is trust and openness in the group.
Dissatisfied   Satisfied
/ 1 / 2 / 3 / 4 / 5 / 6 / 7 /

6. Feel a part of the group.
Dissatisfied   Satisfied
/ 1 / 2 / 3 / 4 / 5 / 6 / 7 /

7. Feel satisfied with how we are using our time.
Dissatisfied   Satisfied
/ 1 / 2 / 3 / 4 / 5 / 6 / 7 /

—I credit this instrument to Robert C. Worley, who used it in a Doctor of Ministry course at the Presbyterian School of Christian Education in Richmond, Virginia.

APPENDIX 2

ATTITUDES TOWARD CHANGE

Score yourself on the following inventory by circling whether you believe the statements are true or false.

	True	False
1. Change takes time to take effect.	T	F
2. Change is impossible in a church system.	T	F
3. The rate of change in the church needs to be slowed.	T	F
4. Change pays dividends to those who plan it.	T	F
5. Churches naturally resist change.	T	F
6. Only massive change is worth the effort.	T	F
7. Churches soon cope with any change.	T	F
8. Change produces growth.	T	F
9. Change is particularly hard for some church members.	T	F
10. Change usually occurs accidentally.	T	F

The preceding instrument will help you analyze your beliefs about change. "True" answers to statements 2 and 10 indicate that you are doubtful about being able to effect change. "True" answers to 1, 5, and 9 show that you are aware of the difficulties in change. "True" answers to 3, 4, 6, 7, and 8 reveal that you need to study the dynamics of change to deepen your understanding of its complexity.

Your answers may disclose that your attitude toward change is quite mixed. Discuss with your board or staff how one's attitude affects one's willingness to instigate and plan change in the church.

APPENDIX 3

HOW ARE WE WORKING TOGETHER AS A STAFF?

Rate on a scale of 1 (lowest in satisfaction) to 7 (highest in satisfaction) the following aspects of your staff relationships:

1. Feel satisfied about the way decisions are made.
   Dissatisfied   Satisfied
   / 1 / 2 / 3 / 4 / 5 / 6 / 7 /

2. Feel there is trust and openness among us.
   Dissatisfied   Satisfied
   / 1 / 2 / 3 / 4 / 5 / 6 / 7 /

3. Feel satisfied about how information is shared.
   Dissatisfied   Satisfied
   / 1 / 2 / 3 / 4 / 5 / 6 / 7 /

4. Feel my opinions matter.
   Dissatisfied   Satisfied
   / 1 / 2 / 3 / 4 / 5 / 6 / 7 /

5. Am satisfied with the way my work is reviewed.
   Dissatisfied   Satisfied
   / 1 / 2 / 3 / 4 / 5 / 6 / 7 /

6. Feel the goals of our staff are clearly defined.
Dissatisfied   Satisfied
/ 1 / 2 / 3 / 4 / 5 / 6 / 7 /

7. Am satisfied with how conflict is resolved.
Dissatisfied   Satisfied
/ 1 / 2 / 3 / 4 / 5 / 6 / 7 /

8. Am pleased with how relationships are nurtured.
Dissatisfied   Satisfied
/ 1 / 2 / 3 / 4 / 5 / 6 / 7 /

9. Feel role expectations are clear and unambiguous.
Dissatisfied   Satisfied
/ 1 / 2 / 3 / 4 / 5 / 6 / 7 /

10. Feel my job description is helpful and clear.
Dissatisfied   Satisfied
/ 1 / 2 / 3 / 4 / 5 / 6 / 7 /

—I modified the material in Appendix 1 so that it would apply to staff relationships.

A SURVIVAL KIT
FOR ASSOCIATE PASTORS

R ank the following items from 1, the least important aspect of ministry for you, to 15, the most important.

YOUR CONCERNS	RANK FOR YOU
1. Too much time with youth work	[ ]
2. Need for more preaching	[ ]
3. More time for family/personal growth	[ ]
4. Too much time on Christian education	[ ]
5. Too much time in visitation	[ ]
6. Not viewed as "real" pastor	[ ]
7. Large gap between salaries	[ ]
8. No regular staff meetings	[ ]
9. Not part of decision-making process	[ ]
10. Lack of open sharing	[ ]
11. Would like to counsel more	[ ]
12. Would like to do more baptisms/weddings	[ ]
13. Would like bigger part in Sunday services	[ ]
14. More authority in church administration	[ ]
15. Lack of secretarial help	[ ]

—Adapted from Marvin Ceynar, "A Survival Kit for Associate Pastors," *Leadership* (Winter 1982): 38. Used by permission.

NOTES

1. Starting Up

1. Roy M. Oswald, *New Beginnings: Pastorate Start Up Workbook* (Washington: The Alban Institute, 1980), 21.
2. Sidney J. Spain, "When the Pastor Moves to a New Parish," *Net Results* (May 1994): 3.
3. Paul M. Dietterich, "Managing Clergy Transition: Start-Up," *The Center Letter* 4 (August 1983).
4. Lyle E. Schaller, "Well, Reverend, What Do You Think?" *Church Management—The Clergy Journal* (February 1985): 37-39. Used by permission

2. Telling Stories

1. I am indebted to Lyman Coleman for this suggestion, but do not know where to locate the source.
2. See particularly James F. Hopewell, *Congregation: Stories and Structure* (Philadephia: Fortress Press, 1987).
3. Carl S. Dudley, *Making the Small Church Effective* (Nashville: Abingdon, 1978), 75, 80.
4. For obvious reasons, I have changed the minister's name and also omitted the name of the church.
5. James P. Wind, quoted in Eugene C. Roehlkepartain, "Your Church's Story," *The Christian Ministry* (March–April 1994): 9. For more, see James P. Wind, *Constructing Your Congregation* (Minneapolis: Augsburg-Fortress Press, 1993).
6. Ibid.

3. Researching Your Congregation

1. University of Dubuque Theological Seminary, Dubuque, Iowa, has placed this advertisement in various publications.
2. See Arlin J. Rothauge, *Sizing Up a Congregation for New Member Ministry* (New York: The Episcopal Church Center, n. d.). See also Lyle E. Schaller, *The Multiple Staff and the Larger Church* (Nashville: Abingdon, 1980); *The Small Church* Is *Different* (Nashville: Abingdon, 1982); *Looking in the Mirror* (Nashville: Abingdon, 1984); and *The Middle-Sized Church: Problems and Prescriptions* (Nashville: Abingdon, 1985).
3. Dudley, *Making the Small Church Effective*, 35.
4. *New Times—New Call: A Manual of Pastoral Options for Small Churches* (Louisville: The Evangelism and Church Development Ministry Unit in Cooperation with the Synod of the Sun, Presbyterian Church [U.S.A.]), 10.
5. Roy M. Oswald, "How to Minister Effectively in Family, Pastoral, Program, and Corporate Sized Churches," *Action Information* (March-April 1991): 3.
6. See Kennon L. Callahan, *Twelve Keys to an Effective Church* (San Francisco: Harper & Row, 1983). For a discussion of these strengths, see especially the "Introduction, Part I: Planning and Hope."
7. Schaller, *The Middle-Sized Church*, 15.
8. Dudley, *Making the Small Church Effective*, 71.
9. Schaller, *The Middle-Sized Church*, 131.
10. Ibid., outside back cover.
11. Rothauge, *Sizing Up*, 31.
12. Oswald, "How to Minister," 6.

4. Testing the Waters Beyond Your Congregation

1. "Getting Started With Your Congregation," (Office for Church Life and Leadership, United Church of Christ, n. d.).
2. For an excellent discussion of open systems, see Jackson W. Carroll, "The Congregation as Chameleon," *Congregations: Their Power to Form and Transform*, C. Ellis Nelson, ed. (Atlanta: John Knox Press, 1988), 46-69.
3. See Jackson W. Carroll, Carl S. Dudley, and William McKinney, eds., *Handbook for Congregational Studies* (Nashville: Abingdon, 1986), for a helpful discussion of this point in chapter 3, especially 48-49.
4. Private correspondence in the personal files of Robert H. Ramey, Jr., Decatur, Georgia.
5. Stanley Hallett, quoted in Roy M. Oswald, *New Beginnings: Pastorate Start Up Workbook*, 54.
6. Ibid.
7. Carl S. Dudley, "The Seven Maps of the Church," *Community Forum* (February 1991): 1, 4.
8. For more on marketing in religious organizations, see Norman Shawchuck et al., *Marketing for Congregations: Choosing to Serve People more Effectively* (Nashville: Abingdon, 1992), 184-207.
9. Hugh Anderson, James Cushman, Henry Snedeker-Meier, Bruce Tischler, and David Wasserman, contributors, *Congregational Mission Studies: Mission Studies Notebook*

(Louisville: Evangelism and Church Development Ministry Unit, Presbyterian Church [U. S. A.], 1989).

10. See Tex Sample, *U. S. Lifestyles and Mainline Churches: A Key to Reaching People in the 90s* (Louisville: Westminster/John Knox Press, 1990). Sample's description of the cultural left, right, and middle forms the background against which I discuss the value of researching lifestyles in the church's social context.

11. Ibid., 104.

12. Ibid., 130-35.

5. Dealing with Conflict

1. See Speed B. Leas, *Discover Your Conflict Management Style* (Washington, D. C.: The Alban Institute, 1984).

2. G. Douglass Lewis, *Resolving Church Conflicts: A Case Study Approach for Local Congregations* (San Francisco: Harper & Row, 1981), 40. See also Daniel Day Williams, *God's Grace and Man's Hope* (New York: Harper and Brothers, 1949), 83-106, for a good discussion of the nature of conflict.

3. Speed B. Leas, *Moving Your Church Through Conflict* (Washington, D. C.: The Alban Institute, 1985), 9.

4. Jack L. Stotts, *Shalom: The Content of the Peaceable City* (Nashville: Abingdon, 1973), 98; quoted in Hugh F. Halverstadt, *Managing Church Conflict* (Louisville: Westminster/John Knox, 1991), 5. See also Halverstadt's discussion in chapter 13 of how Christians should fight for God's *shalom.*

5. Kenneth R. Mitchell, *Multiple Staff Ministries* (Philadelphia: Westminster Press, 1988), 31.

6. Ibid., 32.

7. Ibid., 33.

8. Edwin H. Friedman, *Generation to Generation: Family Process in Church and Synagogue* (New York: The Guilford Press, 1985), 202. See also Charles H. Cosgrove and Dennis D. Hatfield, *Church Conflict: The Hidden Systems Behind the Fights* (Nashville: Abingdon, 1994), 21-23.

9. Murray Bowen, *Family Therapy in Clinical Practice* (New York: Jason Aronson, 1978); quoted in Kenneth R. Mitchell, *Multiple Staff Ministries,* 42.

10. Leas, *Discover Your Conflict Management Style.*

11. See Halverstadt, *Managing Church Conflict,* 21, 22, 202-4 for an excellent discussion of gut theologies.

12. Friedman, *Generation to Generation,* 208.

13. See William H. Willimon, *Preaching About Conflict in the Local Church* (Philadephia: Westminster Press, 1987).

6. Effecting Change

1. See Harold Glen Brown, "Hints on Making Changes," *Leadership* (Spring, 1982) for his practical discussion of several of these changes.

2. See Walter Brueggemann, *Israel's Praise* (Philadephia: Fortress Press, 1988), especially chapter 1, "Praise as a Constitutive Act," in which he talks about how worship can be constitutive as well as responsive.

3. Raymond C. Schulte, "Strategic Planning and Strategic Management for Church Organizations: Strategic Planning as Major Church Re-Orientation," *The Center Letter* 3 (June 1991).
4. Brown, "Hints on Making Changes," 102.
5. "A Declaration of Faith" (1977), *Our Confessional Heritage* (Atlanta: Presbyterian Church in the United States, 1978).

7. Making Friends with Time

1. David Steele, "Busy, Busy, Busy!" *The Presbyterian Outlook*, April 18, 1994, 9.
2. Robert L. Randall, *The Time of Your Life: Self/Time Management for Pastors* (Nashville: Abingdon, 1994).
3. Albert Curry Winn, "Of Time and the Preacher," *The Presbyterian Outlook*, January 11, 1982, 2.
4. "The Pareto Principle," *Leadership Skills for Effective Ministry,* Module 11, Topic 4. To my knowledge The Center for Parish Development never published this module in their notebook on leadership skills.
5. Anthony Arnieri, "Make the Most of Your Time Management," *The Toastmaster* (July 1977): 13-14.

8. Coping with Stress

1. Robert Eliot, quoted in "Stress: Can We Cope?" *Time,* June 6, 1983, 148. Italics mine.
2. Roy M. Oswald, *Clergy Stress and Burnout: A Survival Kit for Church Professionals* (Minneapolis: Ministers Life Resources, 1982), 35-36. Oswald credits John D. Adams for his survey "The Strain Response."
3. Paul M. Dietterich, ed., "Managing Clergy Transition," *The Center Letter* 5 (May 1983). See also Nos. 6-11 for the complete series of 1983 articles.
4. Ibid.
5. Ibid.
6. Ibid.
7. Friedman, *From Generation to Generation,* 269.
8. Ibid., 270.
9. Adapted from Michael G. McBride, "The Vocational Stress of Ministry," *Ministry* (January 1989): 5.
10. Ibid., 6.
11. See William E. Hulme, *Managing Stress in Ministry* (San Francisco: Harper & Row, 1985), 2-4.
12. Ibid., 12.
13. Hans Selye, interviewed by Laurence Cherry, "Straight Talk About Stress," condensed from *Psychology Today* (March 1978): 145. This interview appeared in *Reader's Digest,* n. d.
14. Ibid., 146.

9. Facing Special Start-Up Issues

1. Carol E. Becker, "Women in Church Leadership: An Emerging Paradigm," Norman Shawchuck and Roger Heuser, *Leading the Congregation: Caring for Yourself While Serving the People* (Nashville: Abingdon, 1993), 254.
2. Ibid. Quotation from Sally Helgesen, *The Feminine Advantage: Women's Ways of Leadership* (New York: Doubleday, 1990), 55.
3. See Rensis Likert, *New Patterns of Management* (New York: McGraw-Hill, 1961); Likert, *The Human Organization: Its Management and Value* (New York: McGraw-Hill, 1967); Rensis Likert and Jane Gibson Likert, *New Ways of Managing Conflict* (New York: McGraw-Hill, 1976).
4. Deming, W. Edwards, *Out of the Crisis* (Cambridge: Massachusetts Institute of Technology, 1986).
5. Lynn N. Rhodes, *Co-Creating: A Feminist Vision of Ministry* (Philadelphia: Westminster Press, 1987), 80.
6. Ibid., 120.
7. Celia Allison Hahn, *Growing in Authority, Relinquishing Control* (Washington, D. C.: The Alban Institute, 1994), 74.
8. Rhodes, *Co-Creating*, 81.
9. Ibid., 29.
10. Ibid., 83.
11. Becker, "Women in Church Leadership," 257.
12. Ibid., 259.
13. Hahn, *Growing in Authority*, 74.
14. Becker, "Women in Church Leadership," 266-67.
15. Ibid., 267.
16. See Marvin Ceynar, "A Survival Kit for Associate Pastors," *Leadership* (Winter 1982): 39.

10. Developing as a Minister

1. Donald E. Messer, *Contemporary Images of Christian Ministry* (Nashville: Abingdon, 1989), 25.
2. Ibid., 28.
3. See Messer, *Contemporary Images of Christian Ministry*, for a helpful discussion of these images.
4. I am indebted to colleague John Patton, who introduced me to this teaching method.
5. I first participated in this method of study at an event for pastors of large churches sponsored by The Institute for Advanced Pastoral Studies. See also Jeffrey H. Mahan, Barbara B. Troxell, and Carol J. Allen, *Shared Wisdom: A Guide to Case Study Reflection in Ministry* (Nashville: Abingdon, 1993).
6. At one time the Presbytery of Charleston-Atlantic sponsored such a study group.
7. Richard C. Meyer, *One Anothering: Biblical Building Blocks for Small Groups* (San Diego, Calif.: LuraMedia, 1990), 17.
8. See Roy M. Oswald, *New Beginnings: Pastorate Start Up Workbook*, 49-62, for his discussion of support systems.
9. Adapted from Lyle Schaller, *Survival Tactics in the Parish* (Nashville: Abingdon, 1977), 179-92.
10. Oswald, *New Beginnings*, 52-53.
11. Robert H. Ramey, Jr., "Refueling Pastoral Ministry," *Journeyers* (Spring 1993): 1, 3.

BIBLIOGRAPHY

Anderson, Hugh; James Cushman; Henry Snedeker-Meier; Ruce Tischler; and David Wasserman, contributors. *Congregational Mission Studies: Mission Studies Notebook*. Louisville: Evangelism and Church Development Ministry Unit, Presbyterian Church (U. S. A.), 1989.

Bowen, Murray. *Family Therapy in Clinical Practice*. New York: Jason Aronson, 1978.
Brueggemann, Walter. *Israel's Praise*. Philadephia: Fortress Press, 1988.

Callahan, Kennon L. *Twelve Keys to an Effective Church*. San Francisco: Harper & Row, 1983.
Carroll, Jackson W., Carl S. Dudley, and William McKinney, eds. *Handbook for Congregational Studies*. Nashville: Abingdon, 1986.
Cosgrove, Charles H. and Dennis D. Hatfield, *Church Conflict: The Hidden Systems Behind the Fights*. Nashville: Abingdon, 1994.

Deming, W. Edwards. *Out of the Crisis*. Cambridge, Massachusetts: Massachusetts Institute of Technology, 1986.
Dudley, Carl S. *Making the Small Church Effective*. Nashville: Abingdon, 1978.

Bibliography

Friedman, Edwin H. *Generation to Generation: Family Process in Church and Synagogue.* New York: The Guilford Press, 1985.

Hahn, Celia Allison. *Growing in Authority, Relinquishing Control.* Washington, D. C.: The Alban Institute, 1994.

Halverstadt, Hugh F. *Managing Church Conflict.* Louisville: Westminster/John Knox, 1991.

Hopewell, James F. *Congregation: Stories and Structure.* Philadephia: Fortress Press, 1987.

Hulme, William E. *Managing Stress in Ministry.* San Francisco: Harper & Row, 1985.

Leas, Speed B. *Discover Your Conflict Management Style.* Washington, D. C.: The Alban Institute, 1984.

———. *Moving Your Church Through Conflict.* Washington, D. C.: The Alban Institute, 1985.

Lewis, G. Douglass. *Resolving Church Conflicts: A Case Study Approach for Local Congregations.* San Francisco: Harper & Row, 1981.

Likert, Rensis and Jane Gibson Likert. *New Ways of Managing Conflict.* New York: McGraw-Hill, 1976.

Likert, Rensis. *The Human Organization: Its Management and Value.* New York: McGraw Hill, 1967.

———. *New Patterns of Management.* New York: McGraw-Hill, 1961.

Messer, Donald E. *Contemporary Images of Christian Ministry.* Nashville: Abingdon, 1989.

Meyer, Richard C. *One Anothering: Biblical Building Blocks for Small Groups.* San Diego, California: LuraMedia, 1990.

Mitchell, Kenneth R. *Multiple Staff Ministries.* Philadelphia: The Westminster Press, 1988.

Nelson, C. Ellis, ed. *Congregations: Their Power to Form and Transform.* Atlanta: John Knox Press, 1988.

New Times—New Call: A Manual of Pastoral Options for Small Churches. Louisville: The Evangelism and Church Development Ministry Unit in Cooperation with the Synod of the Sun, Presbyterian Church (U. S. A.), 1991.

Oswald, Roy M. *Clergy Stress and Burnout: A Survival Kit for Church Professionals.* Minneapolis: Ministers Life Resources, 1982.

———. *New Beginnings: Pastorate Start Up Workbook.* Washington: The Alban Institute, 1980.

Randall, Robert L. *The Time of Your Life: Self/Time Management for Pastors.* Nashville: Abingdon, 1994.

Rhodes, Lynn N. *Co-Creating: A Feminist Vision of Ministry.* Philadelphia: The Westminster Press, 1987.

Rothauge, Arlin J. *Sizing Up a Congregation for New Member Ministry.* New York: The Episcopal Church Center, n. d.

Sample, Tex. *U. S. Lifestyles and Mainline Churches: A Key to Reaching People in the 90s.* Louisville: Westminster/John Knox Press, 1990.

Schaller, Lyle E. *Looking in the Mirror.* Nashville: Abingdon, 1984.

———. *The Middle-Sized Church: Problems and Prescriptions.* Nashville: Abingdon, 1985.

———. *The Multiple Staff and the Larger Church.* Nashville: Abingdon, 1980.

———. *The Small Church Is Different.* Nashville: Abingdon, 1982.

———. *Survival Tactics in the Parish.* Nashville: Abingdon, 1977.

Shawchuck, Norman and Roger Heuser. *Leading the Congregation: Caring for Yourself While Serving the People.* Nashville: Abingdon, 1993.

Stotts, Jack L. *Shalom: The Content of the Peaceable City.* Nashville: Abingdon, 1973.

Williams, Daniel Day. *God's Grace and Man's Hope.* New York: Harper and Brothers, 1949.

Willimon, William L. *Preaching About Conflict in the Local Church.* Philadephia: Westminster Press, 1987.

Wind, James P. *Constructing Your Congregation.* Minneapolis: Augsburg-Fortress Press, 1993.